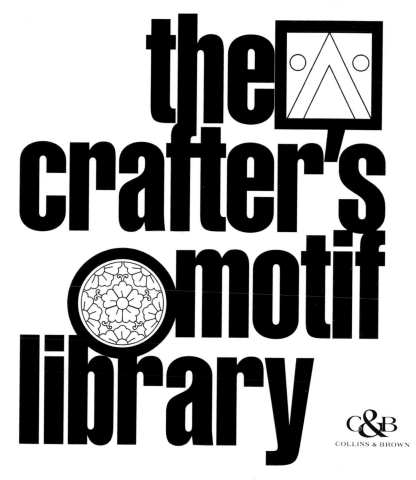

the crafter's motif library

C&B
COLLINS & BROWN

Alan D. Gear & Barry L. Freestone

First published in Great Britain in 2001
by Collins & Brown Limited
London House
Great Eastern Wharf
Parkgate Road
London SW11 4NQ

1 3 5 7 9 8 6 4 2

British Library Cataloguing-in-Publication Data:
A catalogue record for this book
is available from the British Library.

ISBN 1 85585 904 1 (hardback edition)

Conceived, edited and designed by
Collins & Brown Limited

Editor: Kate Haxell
Design: Jonathon Raimes and Kate Haxell
Illustrations: Kuo Kang Chen and Dominic Harris

Reproduction by Global Colour
Printed and bound in Singapore by Tat Wei

INTRODUCTION

A question we are often asked, by all sorts of people interested in all sorts of crafts, is quite simply, 'Where can I find motifs to work from?'. Until now we have had to suggest either ploughing through lots of different magazines and books or drawing your own motifs – something that many people are just not happy to do.

Now, however, we have a perfect answer to that often-asked question: this book, which is packed with over 1,000 different motifs, is exactly what you need. We have put our heads together and chosen motifs that we know are popular and added more from our favourite themes. So, whether you want geometric panels, flowers, children's motifs, dragons, alphabets, or almost anything else, this book has a selection for you to choose from.

The book is broken down into small, specific sections and within those sections every motif is numbered. So, not only is it easy to look up a particular motif, but it is also simple to find it again. The detailed contents list on pages 6-13 will guide you through the different sections in the book.

Each motif is a black-line artwork, ready to be transformed into a wonderful painted, embroidered, knitted, stencilled (the list goes on and on), item, made unique to you by being worked in your own style.

On pages 14-16 you will find some helpful tips for translating the motifs into templates suitable for different crafts. This is a simple process and with so many designs to choose from, we hope that this book will keep you inspired for years to come.

Alan D. Gear and Barry L. Freestone

CONTENTS

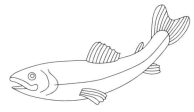

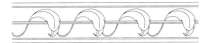

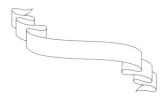

HOW TO USE THIS BOOK

enlarging or reducing a motif

If the motif you have chosen to work with is the size you want your finished design to be, then you can just trace it off in black pen and start work. If, however, you want to use the motif larger or smaller than it is given in the book, you have two options.

photocopying

Enlarging or reducing the motif on a photocopier is the easiest and quickest way of getting it to the size you want.

Divide the size you want the motif to be by the size at which it is given in the book, then multiply the resulting number by 100. This will give you the percentage you need to enlarge or reduce the motif by.

For example, if you want the motif to be 10cm (4in) long and it is given at 7.5cm (3in), then divide 10 by 7.5 to give 1.33 and multiply this by 100 to give 133 per cent.

using a grid

If you do not have access to a photocopier, then you can alter the size of a motif by using the grid method.

Trace off your chosen motif and, with a ruler, draw a grid over it. For a complex motif, make the lines about 5mm (¼in) apart, but for a simpler motif the lines can be up to 5cm (2in) apart.

On a sheet of white paper, draw another grid, with the same number of horizontal and vertical lines, but spacing the lines wider apart to enlarge the motif, or closer together to reduce it. This grid should cover the area that you want the completed motif to fill.

Following the traced-off motif and working in one square of the grid at a time, copy that area onto the larger or smaller grid. When you have finished you will have a motif of the right size ready to work from.

transferring a motif

The process of getting your chosen motif from the pages of this book onto the item you are making varies from craft to craft. However, it is usually quite simple to do. Following are some tips on transferring motifs for some of the most popular crafts.

onto flat glass

Lay the motif underneath the piece of glass and simply outline over the top of it onto the glass.

If you are using black outliner over a black-line motif, you may find it difficult to see where you have outlined and where is still to be done, especially if you are using thick 6mm (¼in) glass. To make everything clearer, use a template in a different colour to the outliner you are using.

If you make a mistake you can try to wipe it off straight away. However, it is more precise, and less messy, to let the outliner dry, then cut the mistake out with a craft knife and re-draw the line with fresh outliner.

onto curved glass

Using scissors, cut out the motif closely, cutting in between the elements of the motif as much as possible, but keeping it in one piece. Place the cut-out motif inside the glass item and, pushing it up against the glass, tape it in position with small pieces of masking tape.

Outline the motif. If you are working on a large glass item, cushion it on a rolled-up piece of fabric or a towel. If the design is right around the item, outline it in sections, letting each section dry before you move on to the next.

onto mirror glass

Lay a sheet of carbon paper face down on the mirror. Lay the motif on top and trace over the lines with a pen or pencil.

Outline the design. When the outliner is dry, wipe off any remaining carbon ink with a cloth.

onto fabric

To transfer a motif onto fabric, place a piece of dressmaker's carbon paper face down on the fabric, lay the motif over the top and run a tracing wheel or pen over the outlines.

If you are embroidering the motif, use both outline stitches and filling-in stitches in your work to give texture.

For appliqué work, cut out the motif allowing a 5mm (¼in) border all around. Tack it in place and then stitch down the edges, using the needle to roll the raw edge under as you work.

onto needlepoint canvas

To transfer a motif onto needlepoint canvas, draw a cross centrally on both the motif and the canvas, then lay the canvas over the motif, lining up the crosses.

Draw over the outlines of the motif onto the canvas with a waterproof pen. If you wish, you can paint in the whole motif with acrylic paints to give a coloured background to work from.

onto cross-stitch linen

Following the instructions for transferring a motif onto fabric, transfer the motif onto a piece of even-weave fabric or waste canvas.

Tack this over the linen and then stitch through both layers. When you have finished the work, carefully pull away the waste canvas, one thread at a time, leaving the embroidered motif in place.

onto a knitting chart

Lay the motif underneath a piece of knitting chart paper. (If you use ordinary graph paper, the motif will distort slightly when it is knitted up as knit stitches are wider than they are tall). Following the outlines of the motif, mark the appropriate squares on the chart paper. If you want to use different colours in the knitted motif, use coloured pens to mark in the squares

Use the resulting chart in conjunction with a knitting pattern, reading the chart from left to right for a knit row and from right to left for a purl row.

If you are working Swiss darning onto a piece of knitted fabric, transfer the motif onto a chart as described above. Following the chart, work the first row from right to left, then the second row from left to right. Continue working in alternate directions until the design is completed.

onto paper for découpage

Photocopy the motifs onto plain paper and decorate them with paints or pencils. Seal them with PVA adhesive (diluted one part PVA to two parts water) before using them.

Alternatively, photocopy the motifs onto coloured or patterned paper, then just cut them out.

onto stencil card

Lay a piece of carbon paper face down on the card, lay the motif on top and trace over the outlines with a pen.

Alternatively, scribble over the lines on the back of the motif with a soft pencil, lay it face up on the card and trace over the outlines.

onto a sponge stamp

Lay the sponge on a cutting mat and tape the motif to the top of it. Using a sharp craft knife, cut around the outlines of the motif, cutting through the paper and the sponge.

It is usually easier to use the stamp if you glue it onto a backing of thick card or thin wood first.

1.flowers

1a.1

1a.2

1a.3

1a.4

1a.5

1a.7

1a.6

1b.1

1b.2

1b.3

1b.4

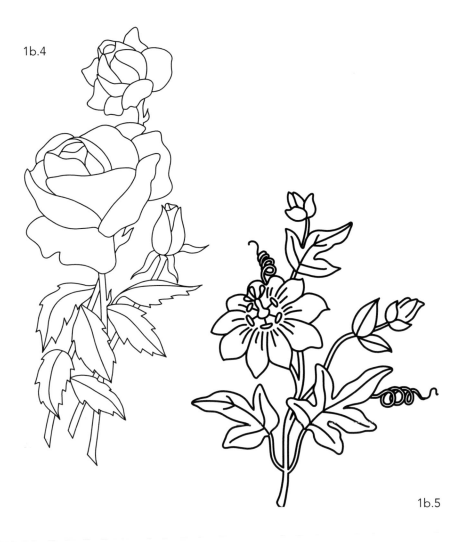

1b.5

1b.6

1b.7

1b.8

1b.9

1c.1

1c.2

1c.3

1c.4

1c.5

1c.6

1c.7

1c.8

1c.9

1c.10

1c.11

1c.12

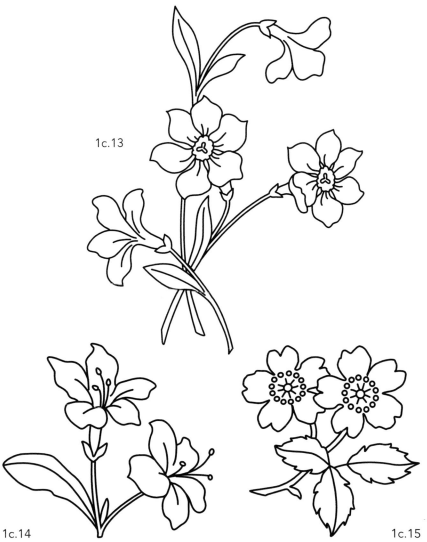

1c.13

1c.14

1c.15

1c.16

1c.17

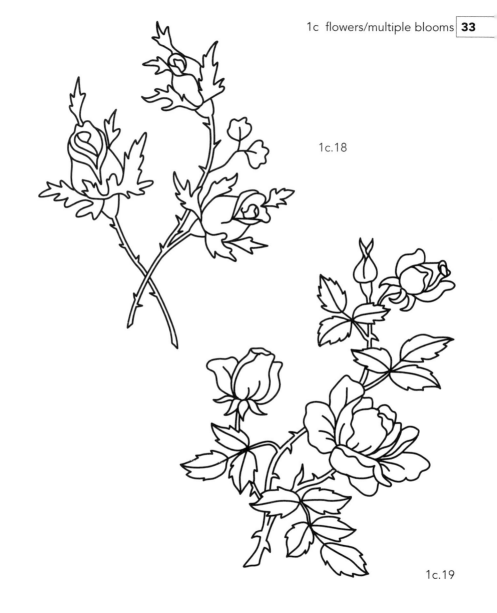

1c.18

1c.19

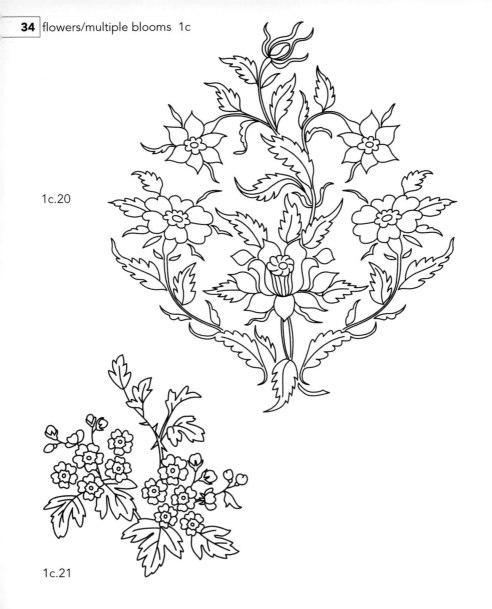

1c.20

1c.21

1c.22

1c.23

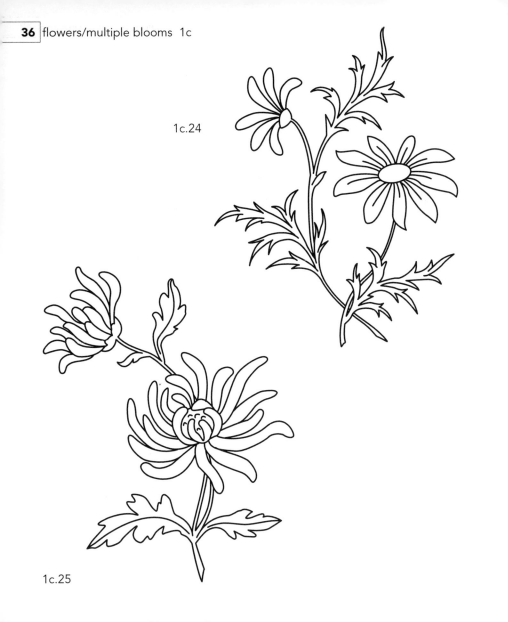

1c.24

1c.25

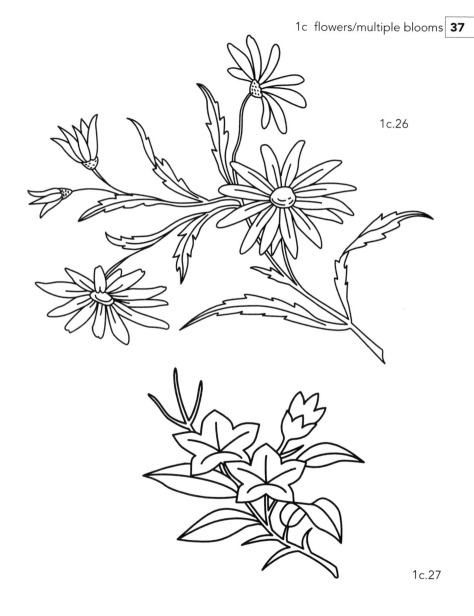

1c.26

1c.27

1c.28

1c.29

1c.30

1c.31

1c.32

1c.33

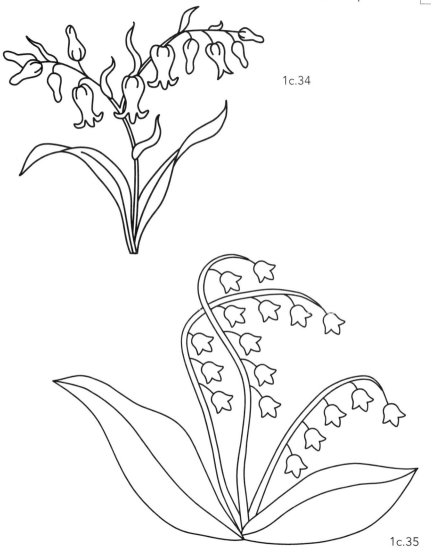

1c.34

1c.35

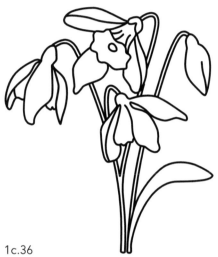

1c.36

1c.37

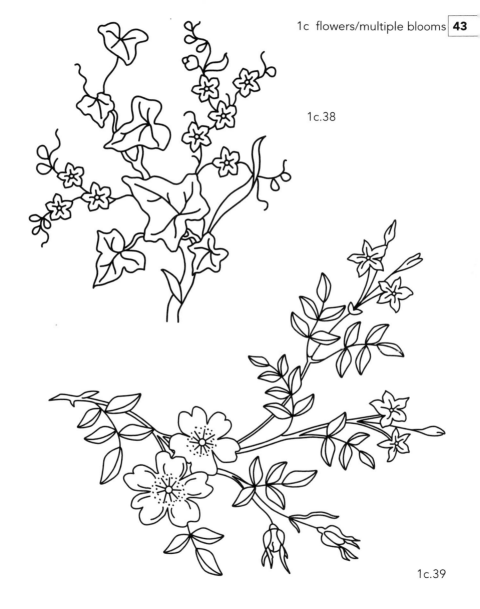

1c.38

1c.39

1c.40

1c.41

1d.1

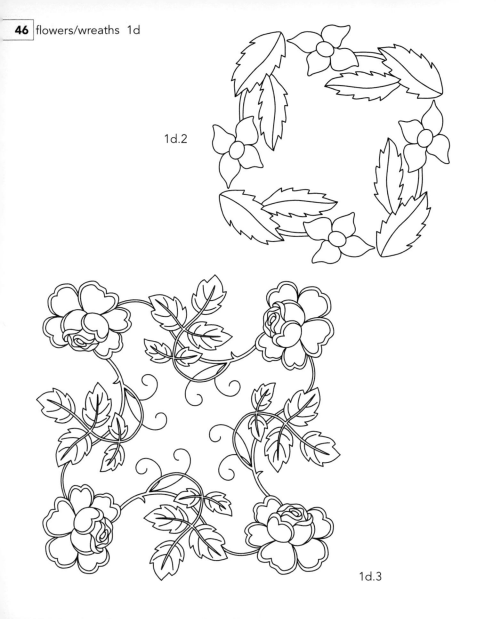

1d.2

1d.3

1d.4

1d.5

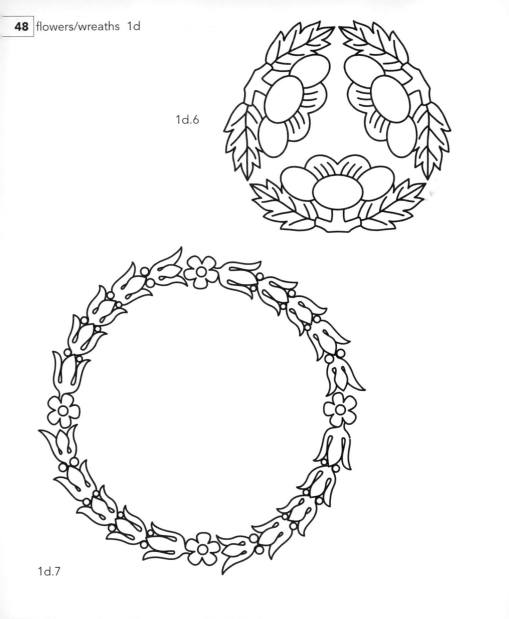

1d.6

1d.7

1e.1

1e.2

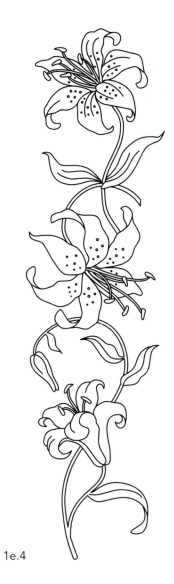

1e.3

1e.4

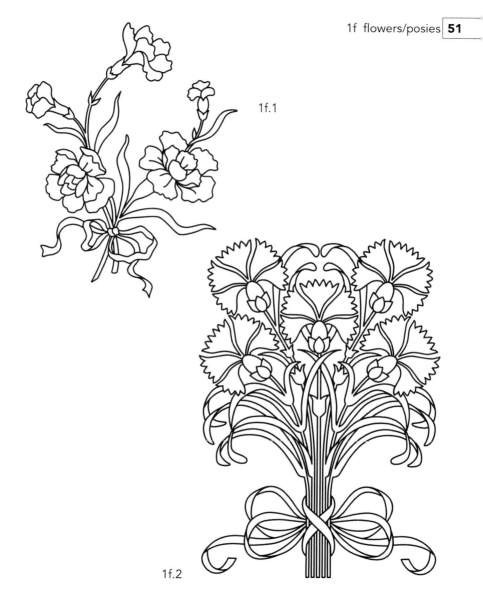

1f.1

1f.2

1g.1

1g.2

1g.3

1g.4

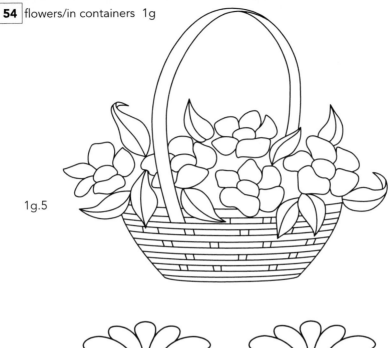

1g.5

1g.6

1g.7

1g.8

1g.9

1g.10

1g.11

1g.12

1g.14

1g.13

1g.15

1h.1

1h.2

1h.3

1h.4

1h.5

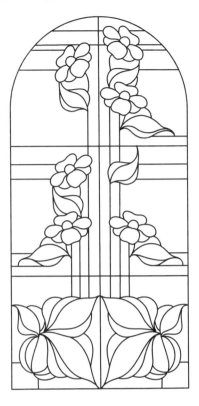

1h.6

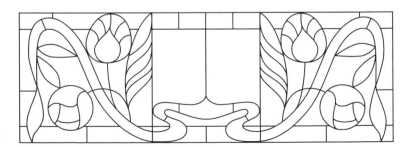

1h.7

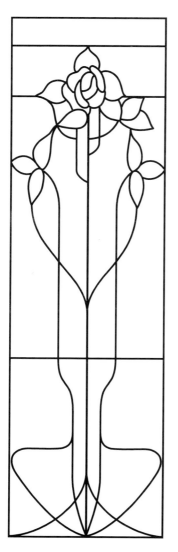

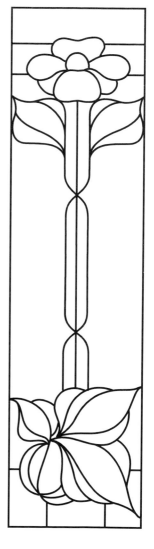

1h.8   1h.9

1h.10

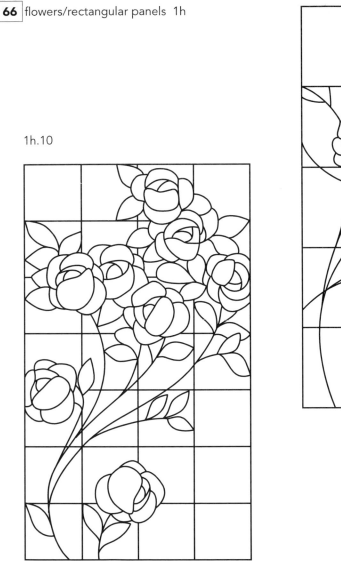

1h.11

1h.12

1h.13

1h.14

1h.15

1h.16

1h.17

1h.18

1i.1

1i.2

1i.3

1i.4

1i.5

1i.7

1i.8

1i.9

1i.10

1i.11

1i.12

1i.13

1j.1

1j.2

1k.1

1k.2

1k.3

1k.4

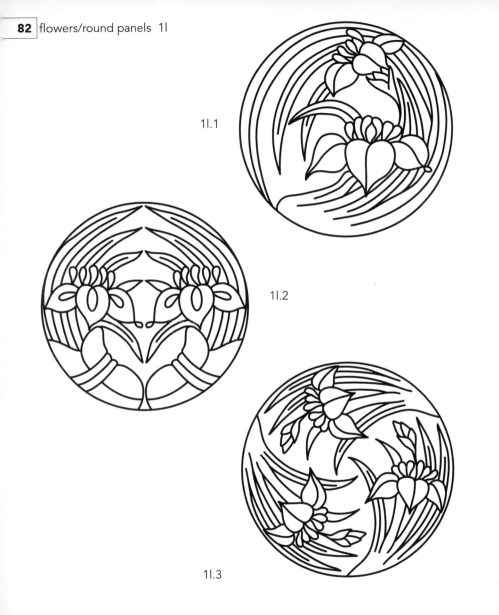

1l.1

1l.2

1l.3

11.4

11.5

11.6

1l.7

1l.8

1l.9

1l.10

1l.11

1l.12

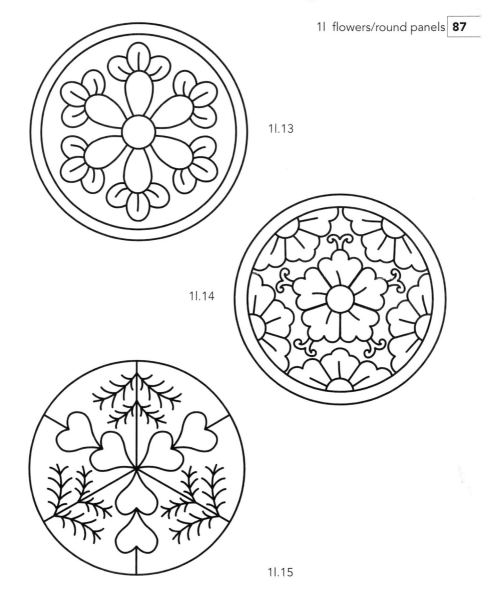

1l.13

1l.14

1l.15

1l.16

1l.17

1l.18

1l.19

1l.20

1l.21

1l.22

1l.23

1l.24

1m.1

1m.2

1m.3

1m.4

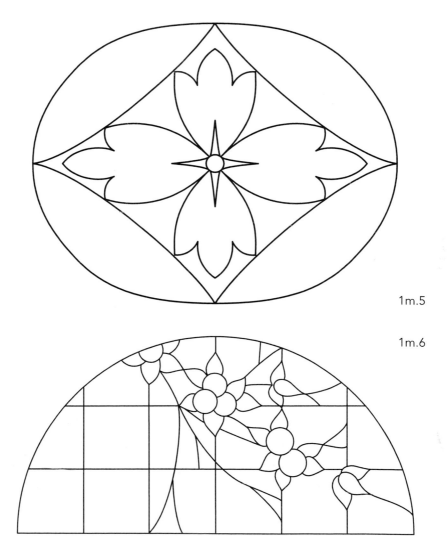

1m.5

1m.6

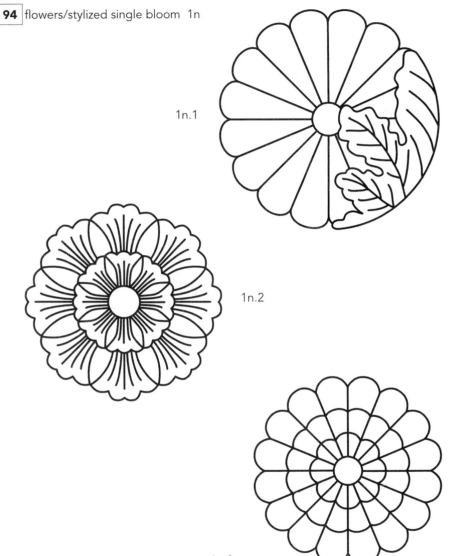

1n.1

1n.2

1n.3

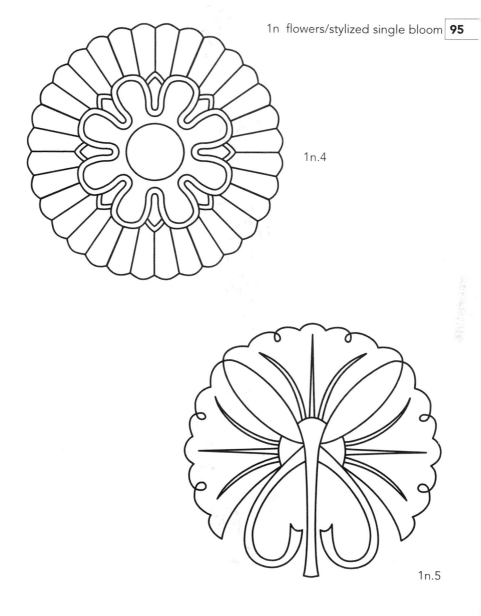

1n.4

1n.5

1n.6

1n.7

1n.8

1n.9

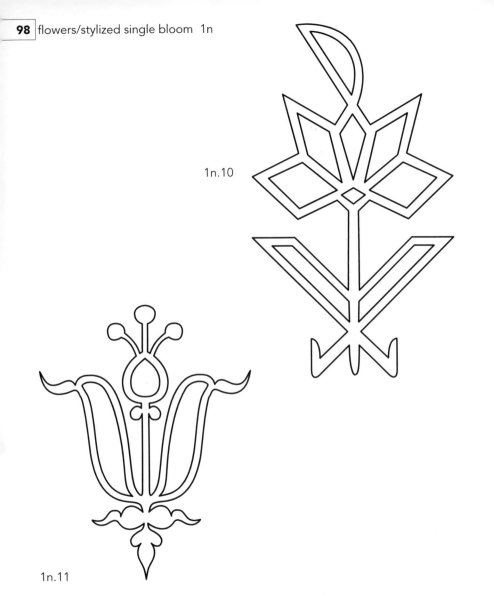

1n.10

1n.11

1n.12

1n.13

1n.14

1n.15

1n.16

1n.17

1n.18

1n.19

1n.20

1n.21

1n.22

1o.1

1o.2

1o.3

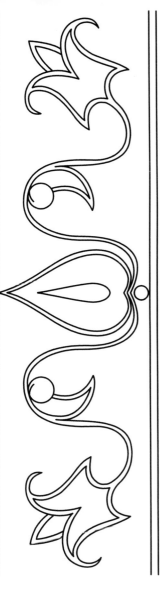

1o.4

1o.5

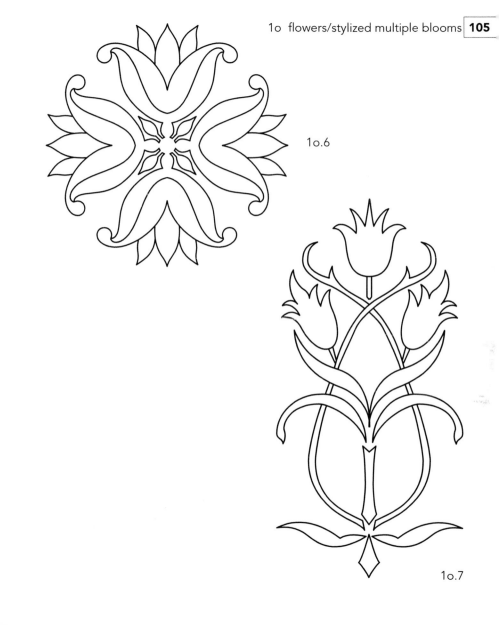

1o.6

1o.7

1o.8

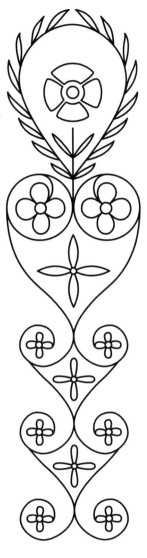

1o.9

1o.10

1o.11

1o.12

1o.13

1o.14

1o.15

1o.16

1o.17

1o.18

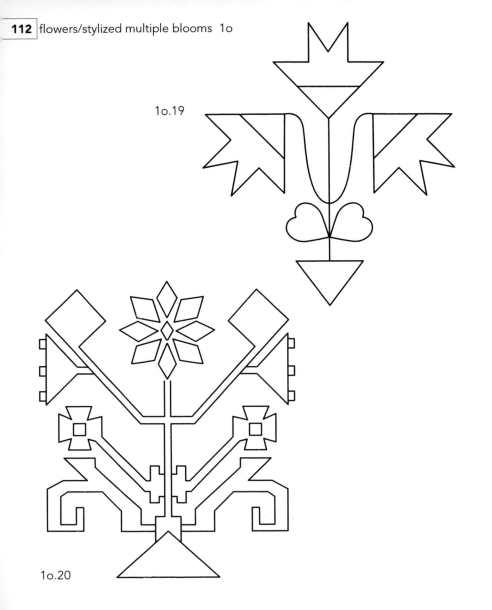

1o.19

1o.20

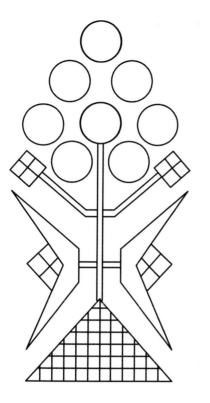

1o.21

1o.22

2.foliage

2a.1

2a.2

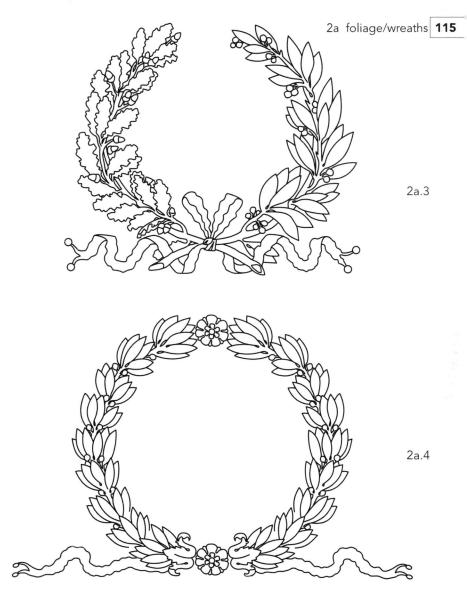

2a.3

2a.4

2a.5

2a.6

2a.7

2a.8

2a.9

2a.10

2b.1

2b.2

2b.3

2b.4

2c.1

2c.2   2c.3

2c.4

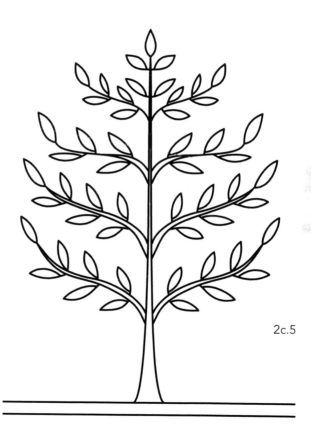

2c.5

2d.1

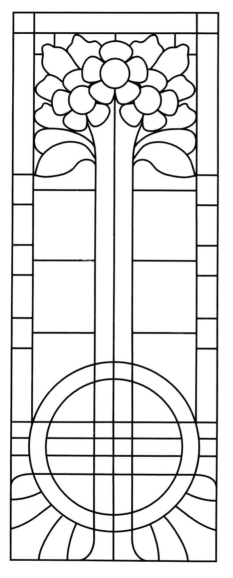

2d.2   2d.3

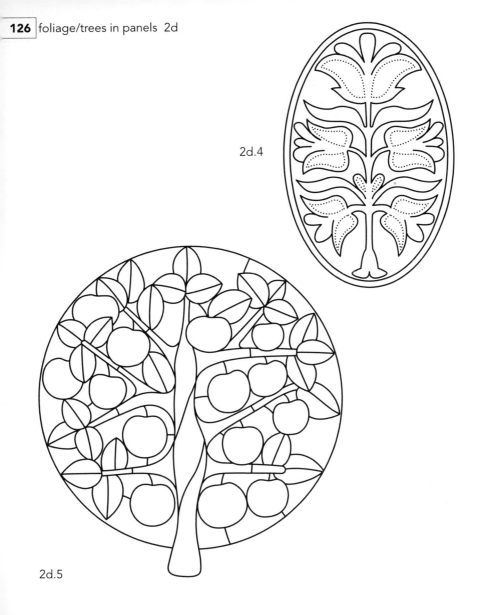

2d.4

2d.5

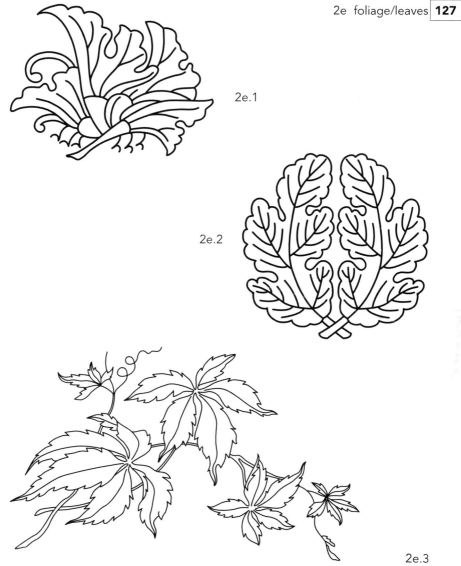

2e.1

2e.2

2e.3

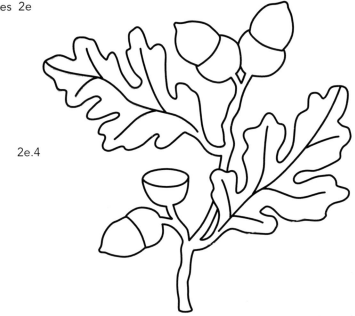

2e.4

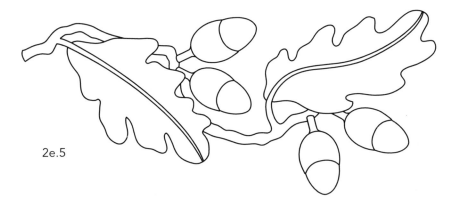

2e.5

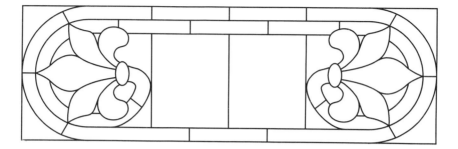

2f.1

2f.2

2f.3

2f.4

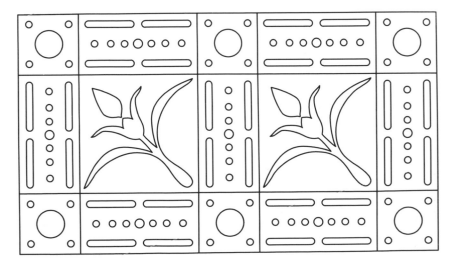

2g.1

2g.2

2g.3

2g.4

2h.1

2h.2

2h.3

2h.4

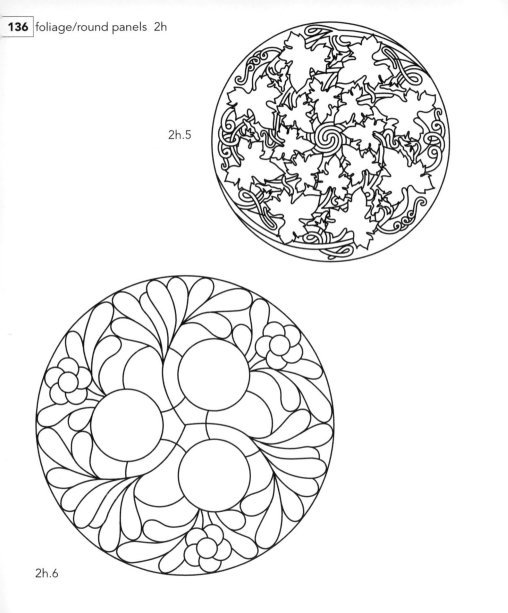

2h.5

2h.6

2i.1

2i.2

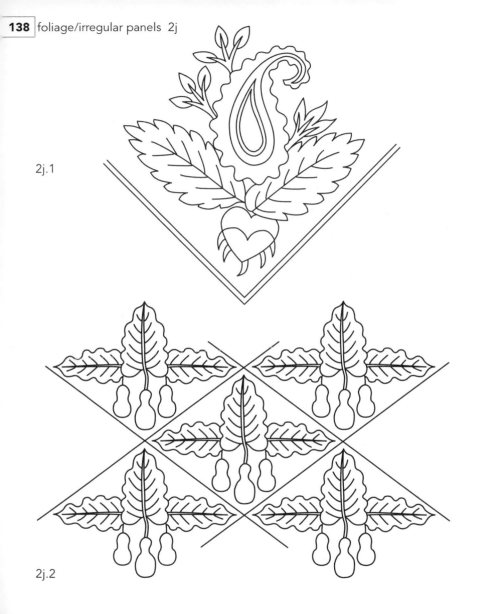

2j.1

2j.2

2j.3

2k.1

2k.2

2k.3

2k.4

2k.5

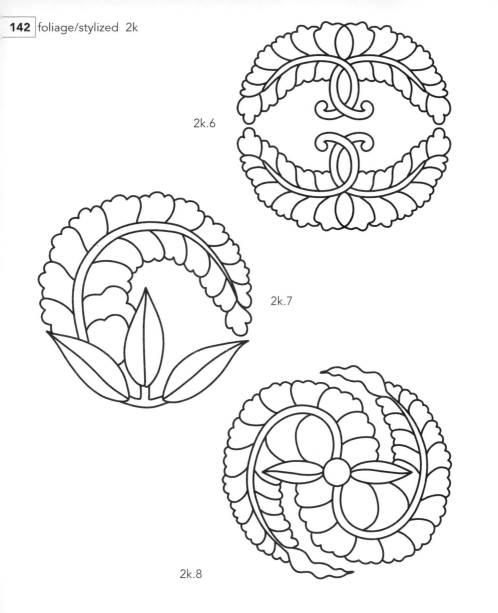

2k.6

2k.7

2k.8

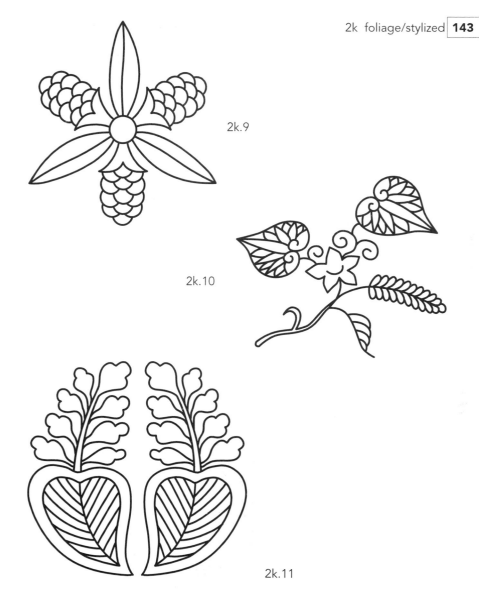

2k.9

2k.10

2k.11

2k.12

2k.13

2k.14

2k.15

2k.16

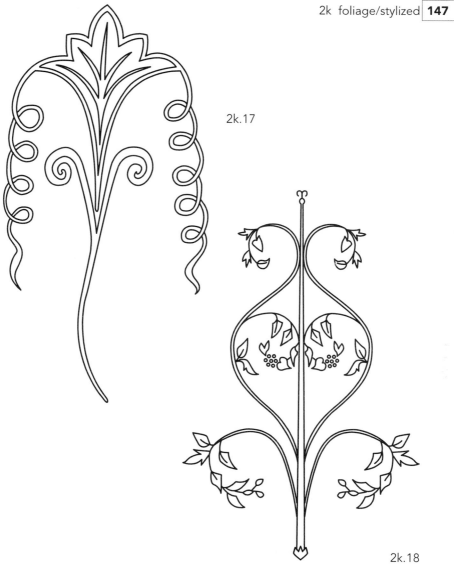

2k.17

2k.18

2k.19

2k.20

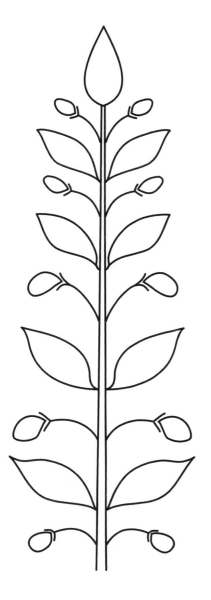

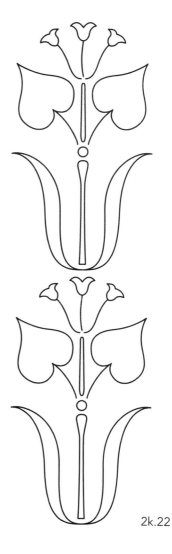

2k.21

2k.22

3.figures

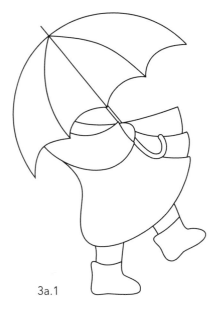

3a.1

3a.2

3a.3

3a.4

3a.5

3b.1

3b.2

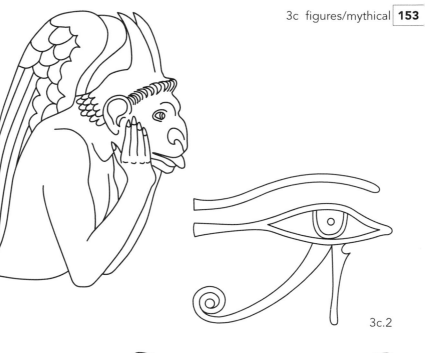

3c.1

3c.2

3c.3

3d.1

3d.2

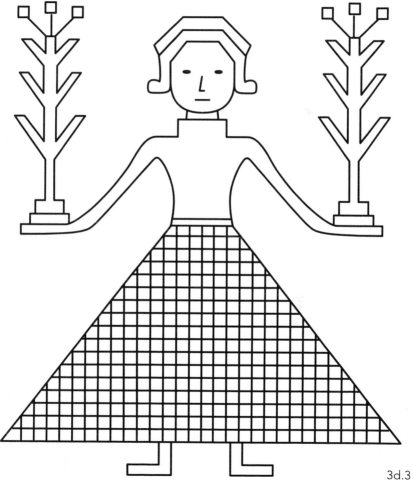

3d.3

3e.1

3e.2

3e.3

3e.4

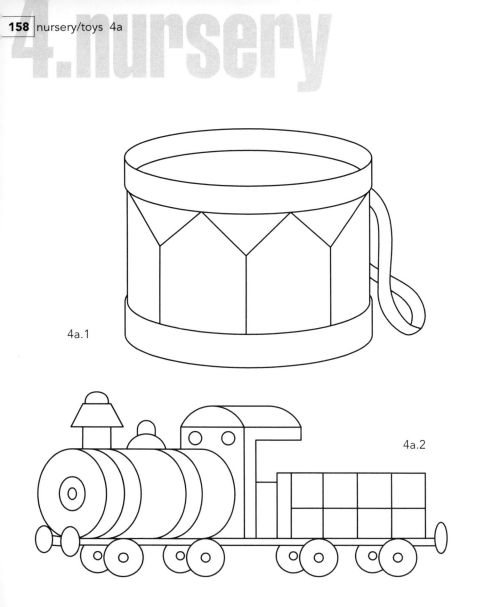

4a.1

4a.2

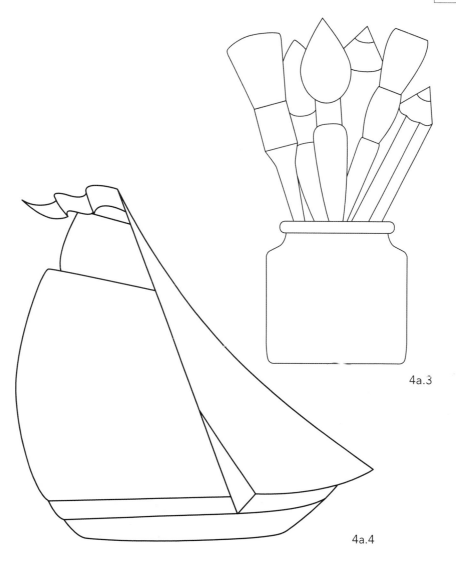

4a.3

4a.4

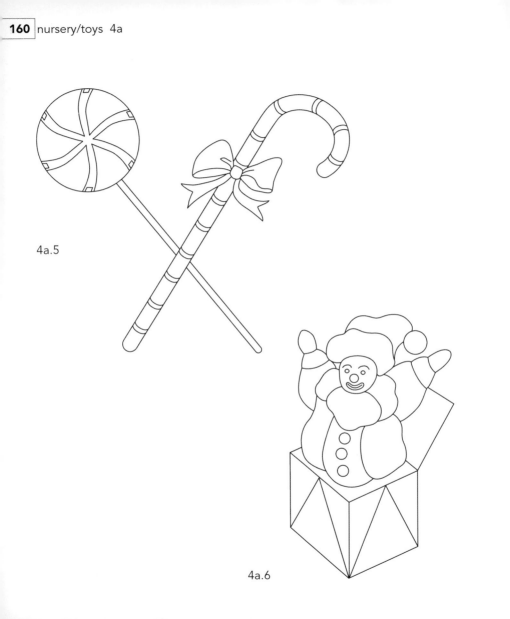

4a.5

4a.6

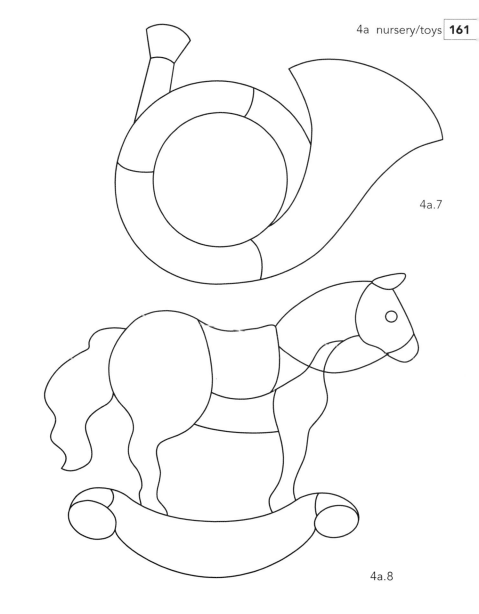

4a.7

4a.8

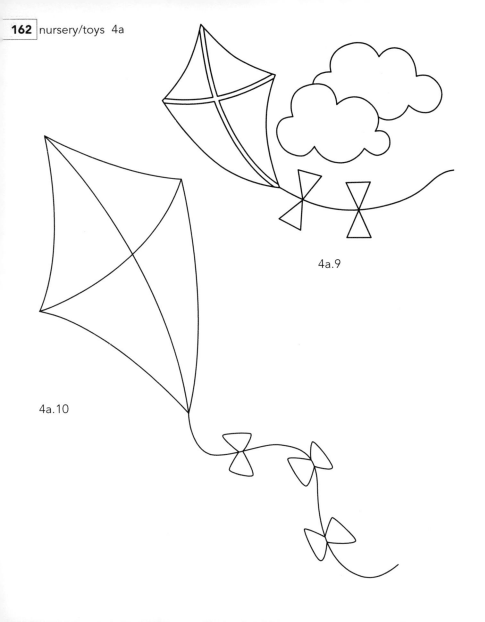

4a.9

4a.10

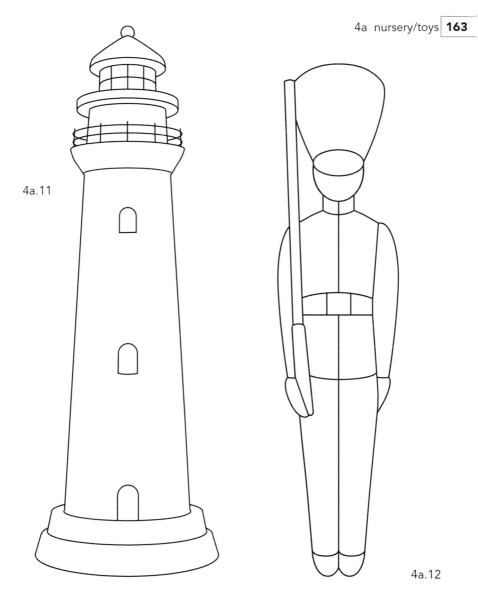

4a.11

4a.12

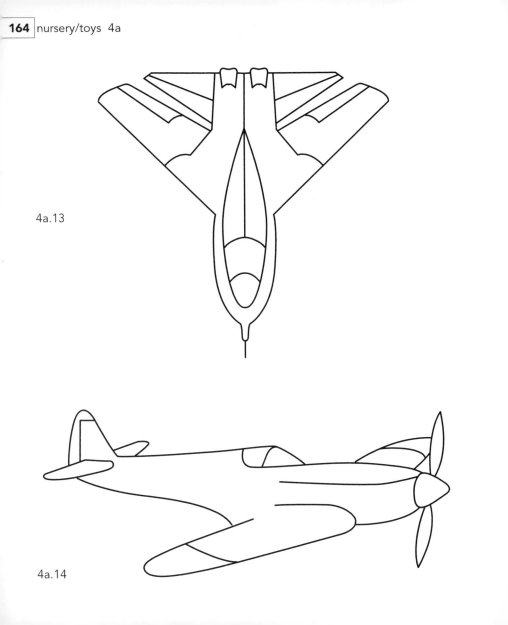

4a.13

4a.14

4a.15

4a.16

4b.1

4b.2

4b.3

4b.4

4c.1

4c.2

4c.3

4c.4

4c.5

4d.1

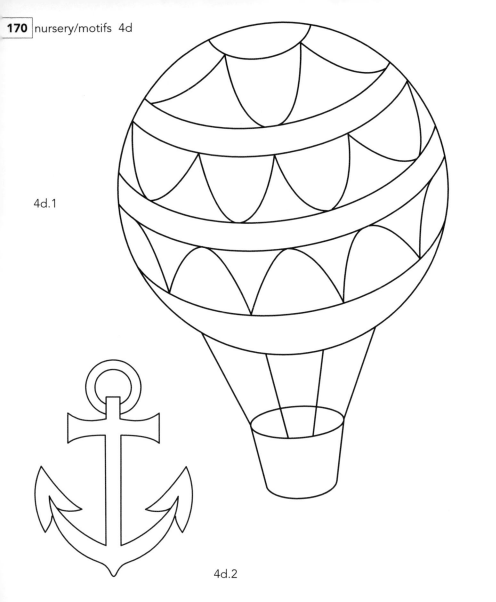

4d.2

4d.3

4d.4

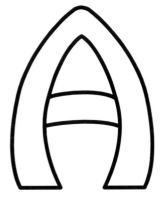

5a.1

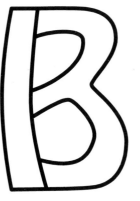

5a.2

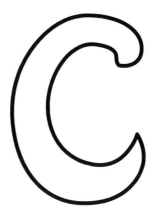

5a.3

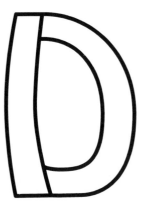

5a.4

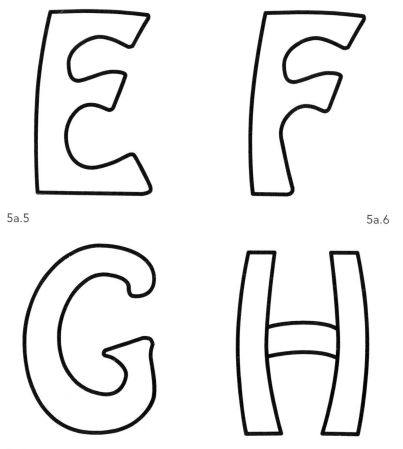

5a.5

5a.6

5a.7

5a.8

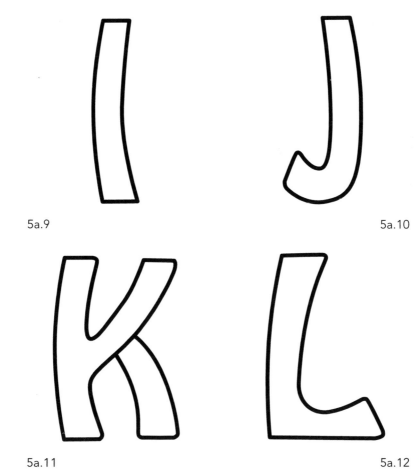

5a.9

5a.10

5a.11

5a.12

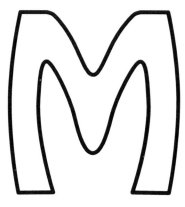

5a.13

5a.14

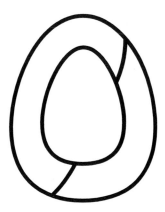

5a.15

5a.16

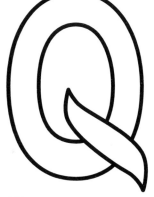

5a.17

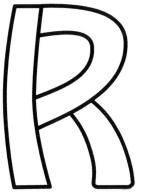

5a.18

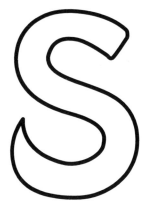

5a.19

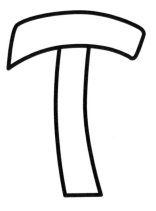

5a.20

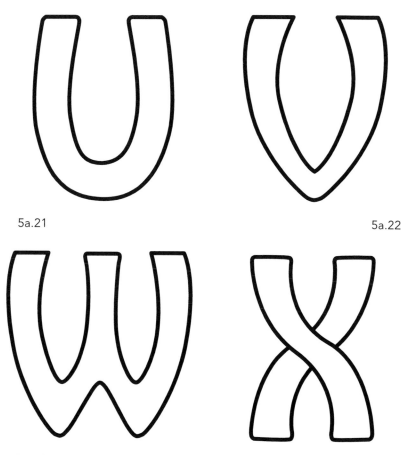

5a.21

5a.22

5a.23

5a.24

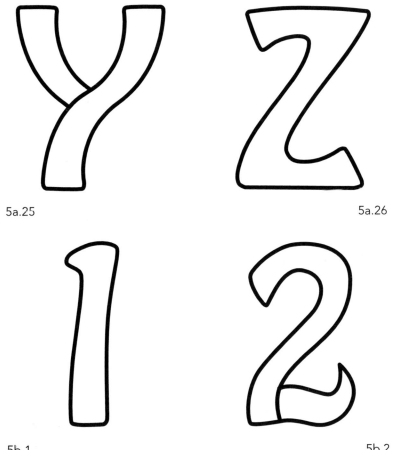

5a.25

5a.26

5b.1

5b.2

5b.3

5b.4

5b.5

5b.6

5b.7

5b.8

5b.9

5b.10

5c.1

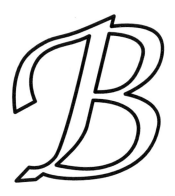

5c.2

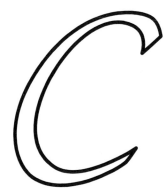

5c.3

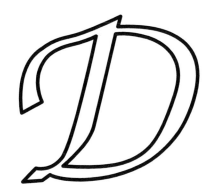

5c.4

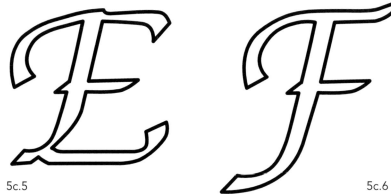

5c.5

5c.6

5c.7

5c.8

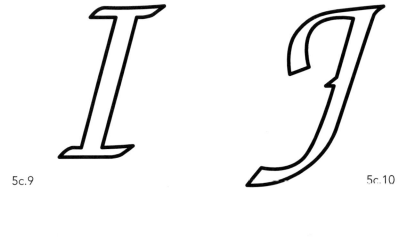

5c.9

5c.10

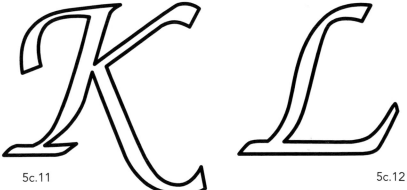

5c.11

5c.12

5c.13

5c.14

5c.15

5c.16

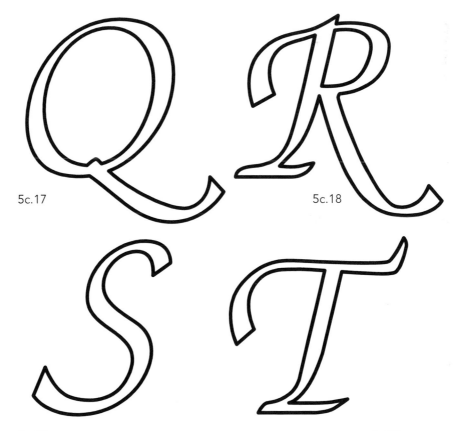

5c.17

5c.18

5c.19

5c.20

5c.21

5c.22

5c.23

5c.24

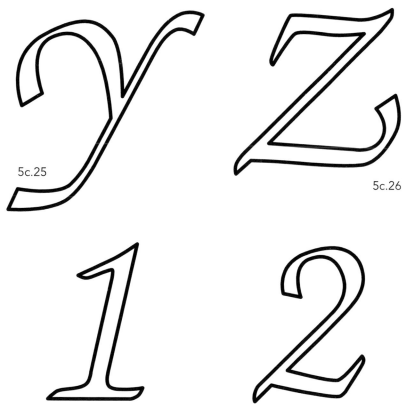

5c.25

5c.26

5d.1

5d.2

5d.3

5d.4

5d.5

5d.6

5d.7

5d.8

5d.9

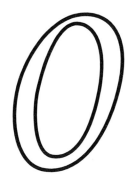

5d.10

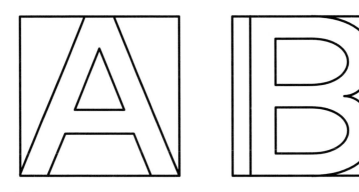

5e.1

5e.2

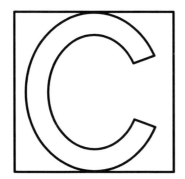

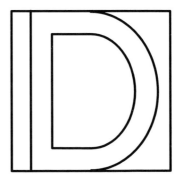

5e.3

5e.4

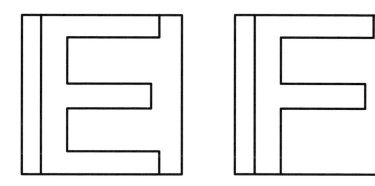

5e.5

5e.6

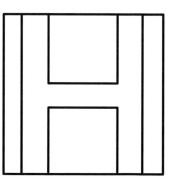

5e.7

5e.8

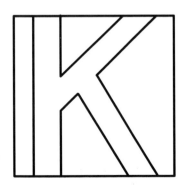

5e.9

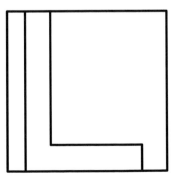

5e.10

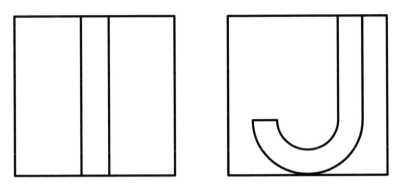

5e.11

5e.12

5e.13

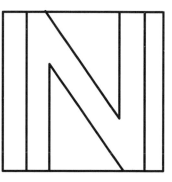

5e.14

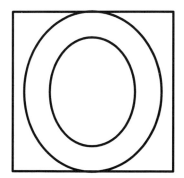

5e.15

5e.16

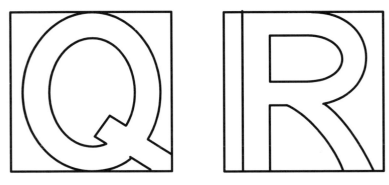

5e.17

5e.18

5e.19

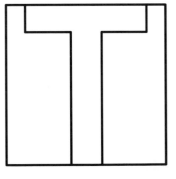

5e.20

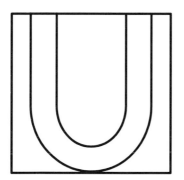

5e.21

5e.22

5e.23

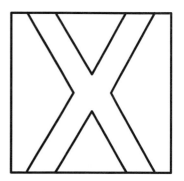

5e.24

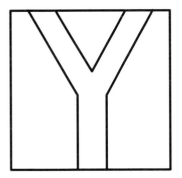

5e.25

5e.26

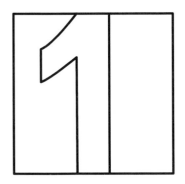

5f.1

5f.2

5f.3

5f.4

5f.5

5f.6

5f.7

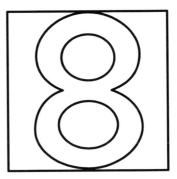

5f.8

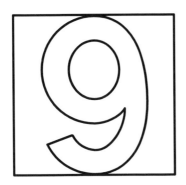

5f.9

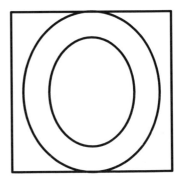

5f.10

If you are outlining lettering onto the back of a piece of glass then you will need to reverse the letters, so that when they are seen from the front they are the right way round. To do this, photocopy the letters you want to outline, lay them face down on a sheet of white paper and trace over the back of the lines with a pen. The result should look like the letters on this page.

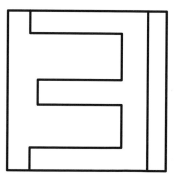

5g.1

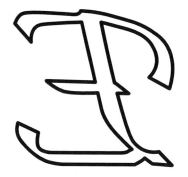

5g.2

5g.3

6a.1

6a.2

6a.3

6b.1

6b.2

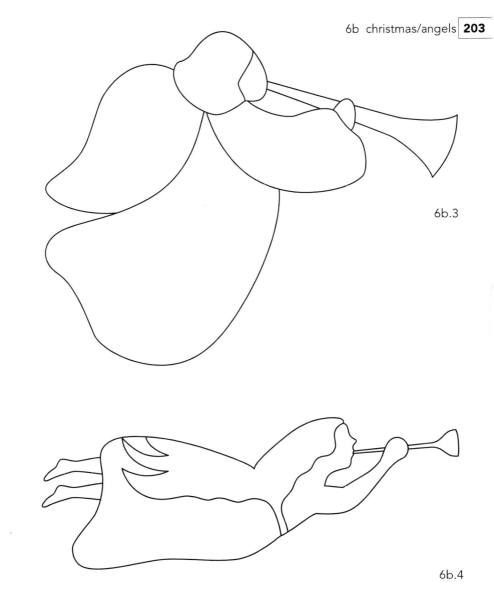

6b.3

6b.4

6b.5

6b.6

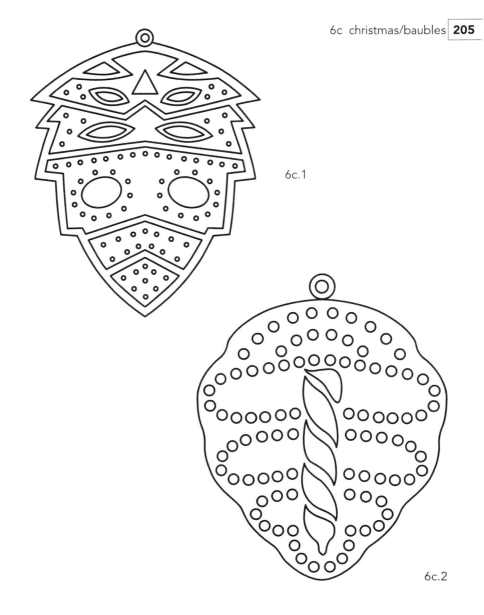

6c.1

6c.2

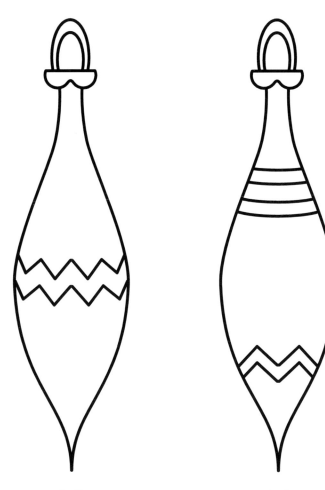

6c.3   6c.4

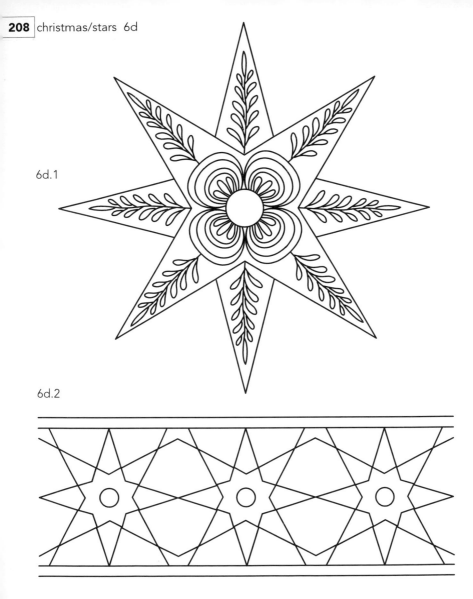

6d.1

6d.2

6d.3

6d.4

6e.1

6e.2

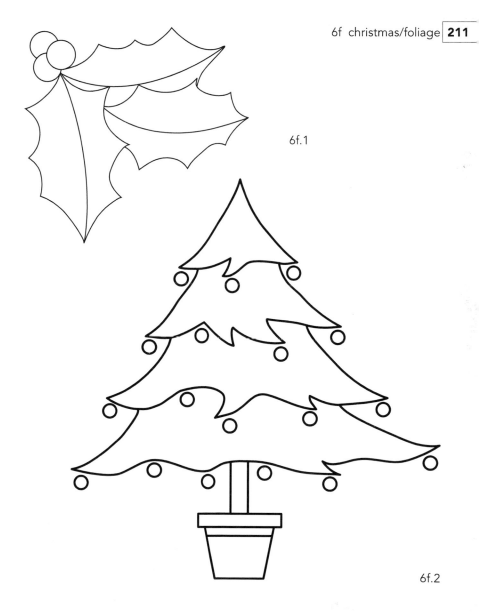

6f.1

6f.2

6g.1

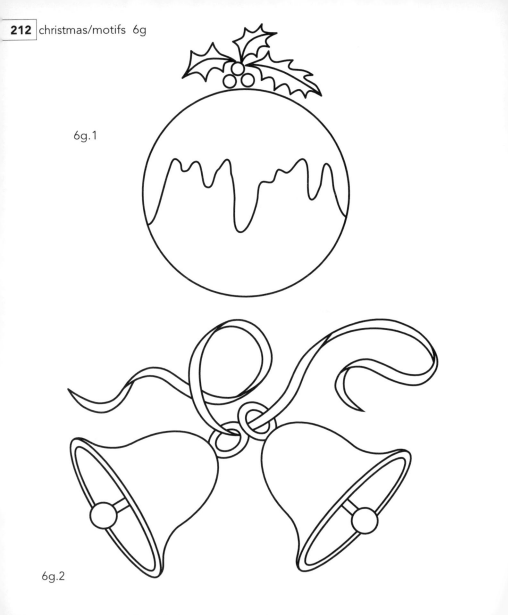

6g.2

6g.3

6g.4

7.valentine

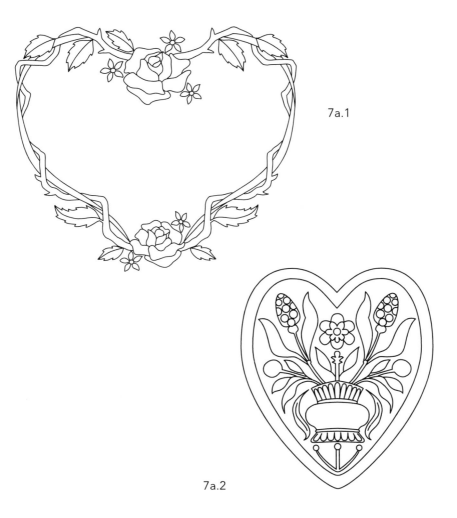

7a.1

7a.2

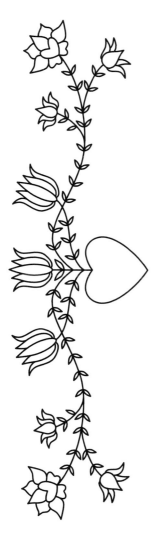

7a.3

7a.4

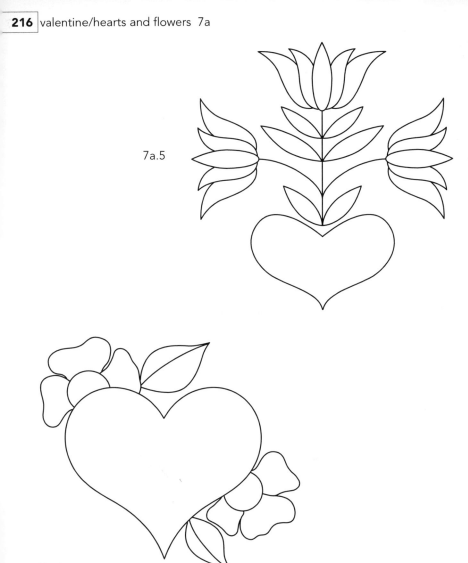

7a.5

7a.6

7b.1

7b.2

7b.3

7c.1

7c.2

7d.1

7d.2

7e.1

7e.2

7e.3

7e.4

8.easter

8a.1

8a.2

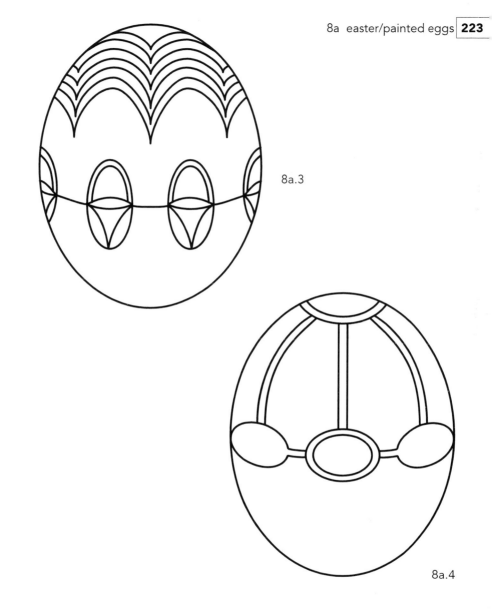

8a.3

8a.4

8a.5

8a.6

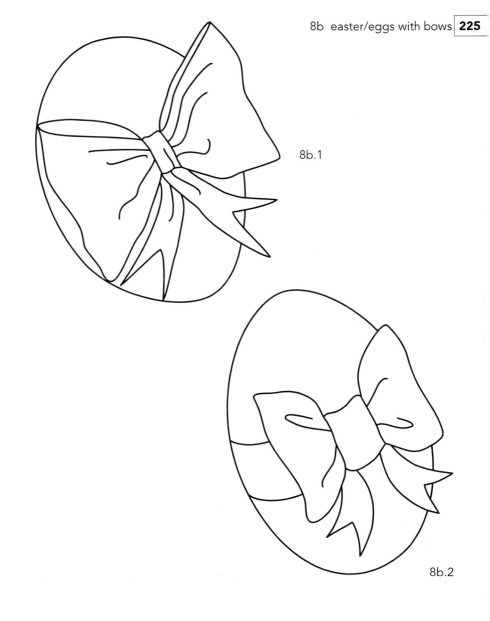

8b.1

8b.2

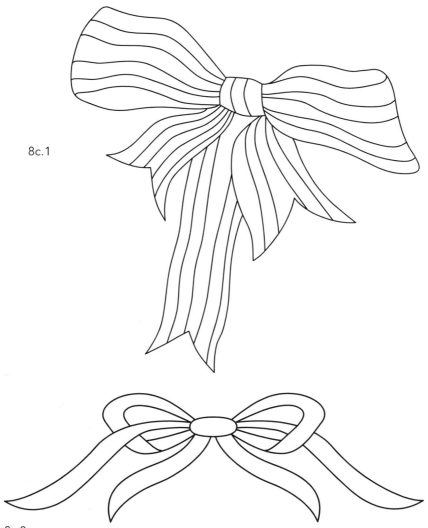

8c.1

8c.2

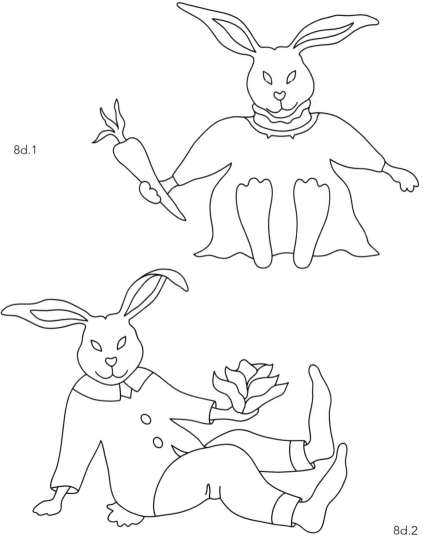

8d.1

8d.2

9.celestial

9a.1

9a.2

9a.3

9b.1

9b.2

9b.3

9b.4

9b.5

9b.6

9c.1

9c.2

9c.3

9c.4

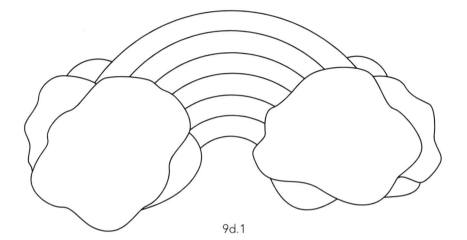

9d.1

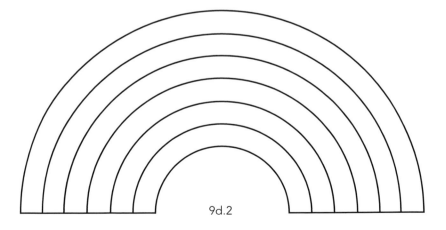

9d.2

9e.1

9e.2

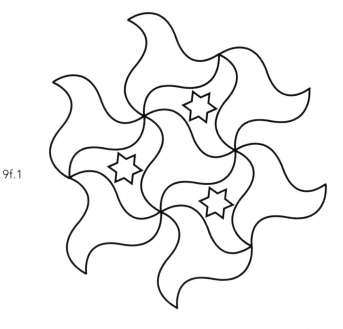

9f.1

9f.2

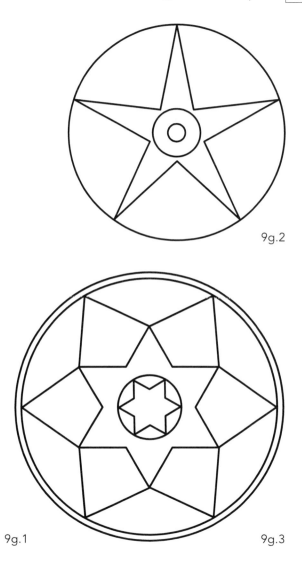

9g.2

9g.1

9g.3

10a.1

10a.2

10a.3

10b.1

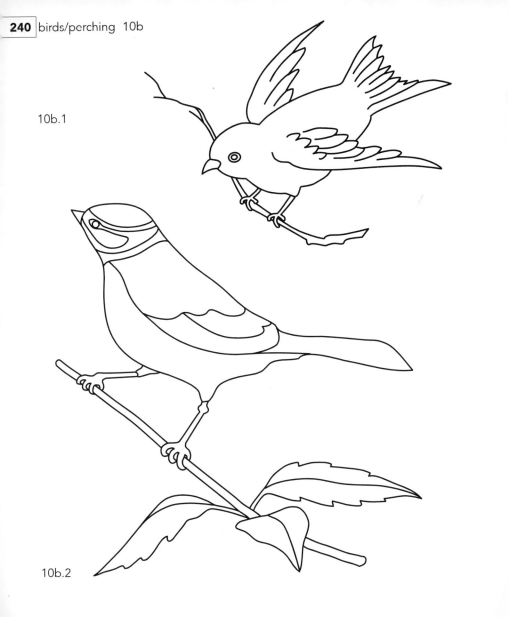

10b.2

10b.3

10b.4

10c.1

10c.2

10c.3

10c.4

10d.1

10d.2

10d.3

10e.1

10e.2

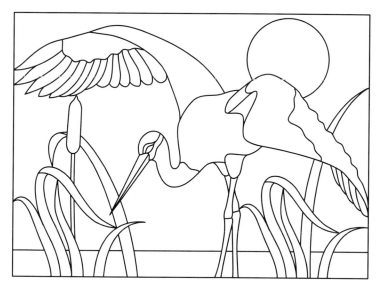

10e.3

10e.4

10e.5

10e.6

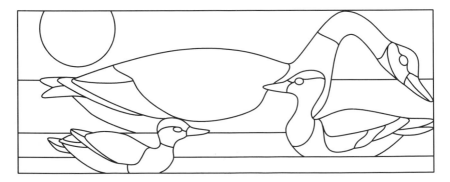

10f.1

10f.2

10f.3

10f.4

10f.5

10f.6

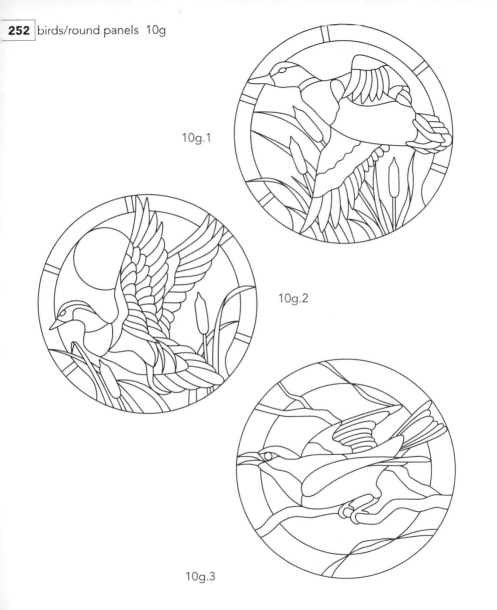

10g.1

10g.2

10g.3

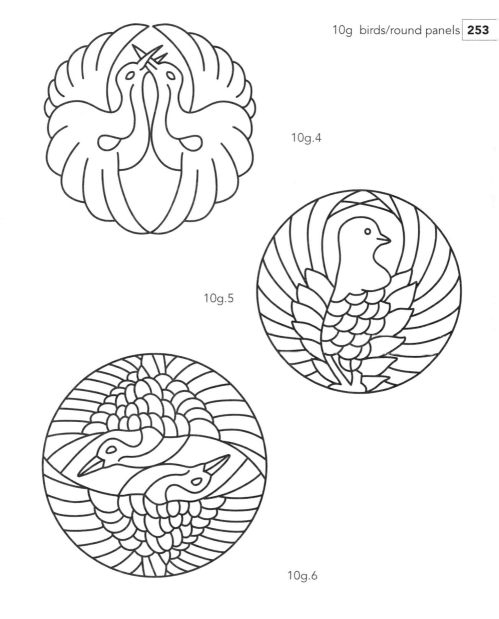

10g.4

10g.5

10g.6

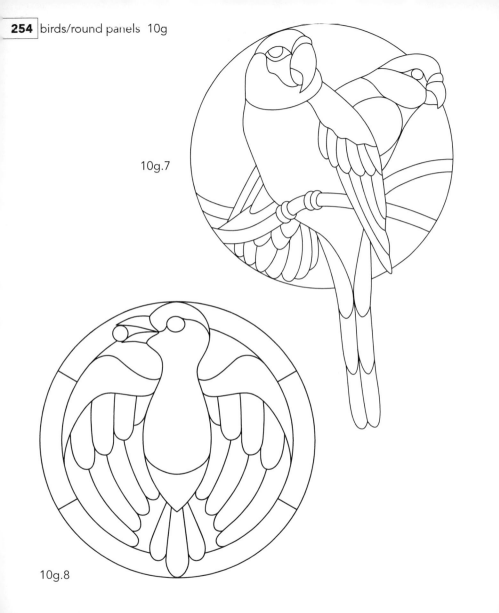

10g.7

10g.8

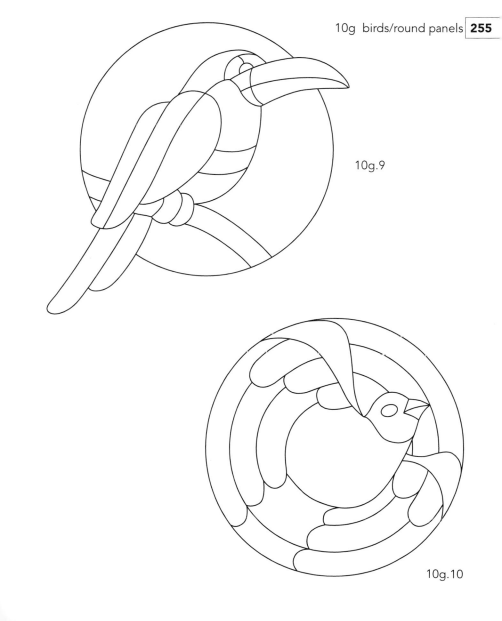

10g.9

10g.10

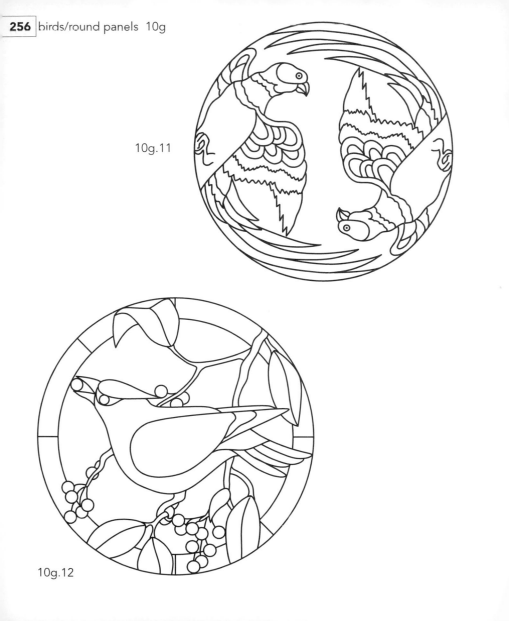

10g.11

10g.12

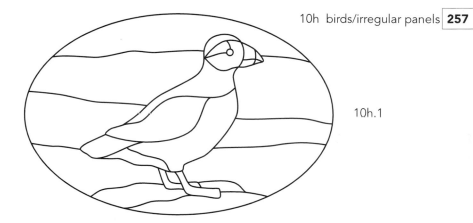

10h.1

10h.2

10h.3

10h.4

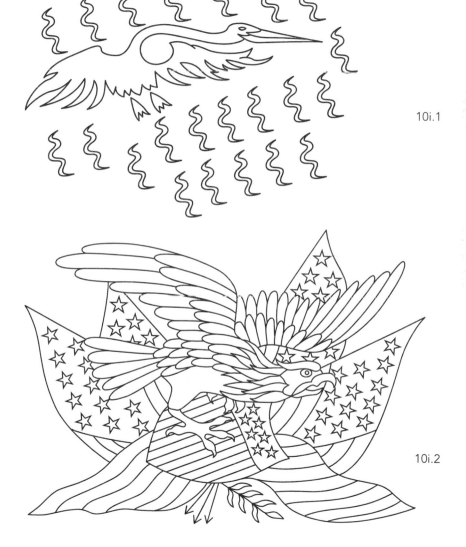

10i.1

10i.2

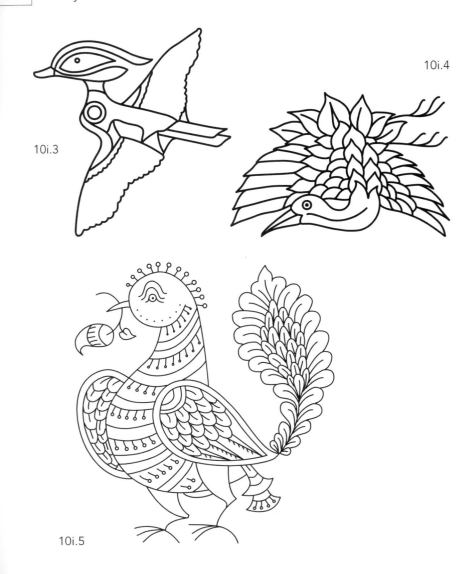

10i.4

10i.3

10i.5

10i.6

10i.7

10i.8

10i.9

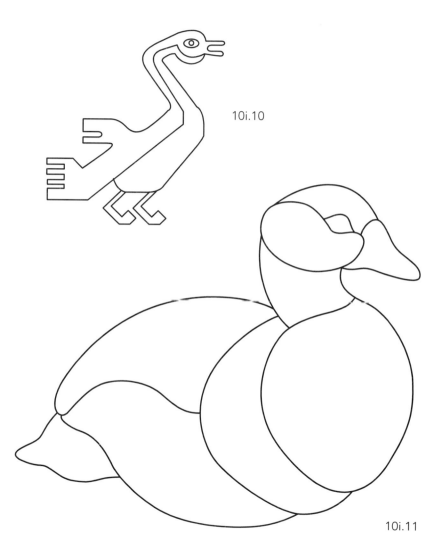

10i.10

10i.11

10j.1

10j.2

10j.3

10j.4

10k.1

10k.2

10k.3

10k.4

10k.5

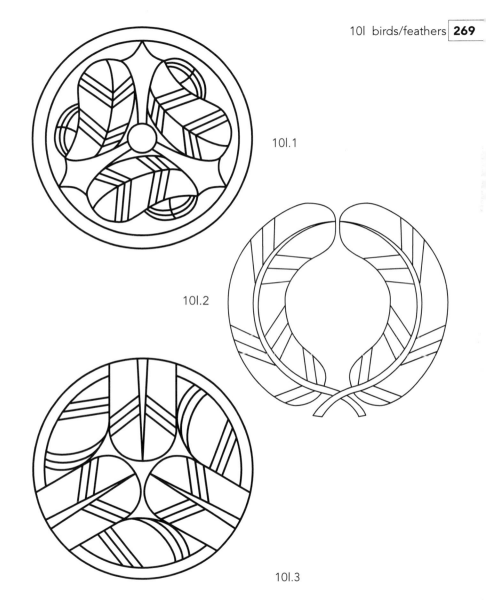

10l.1

10l.2

10l.3

11.insects

11a.1

11a.2

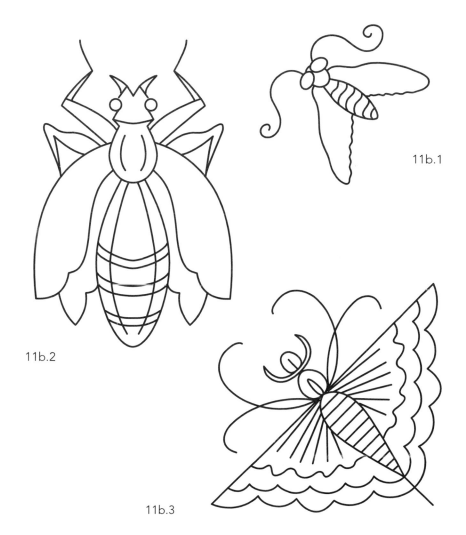

11b.1

11b.2

11b.3

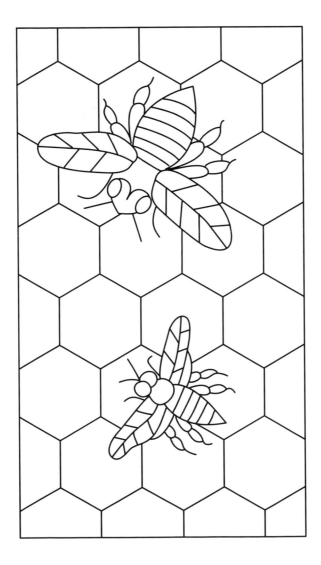

11c.1

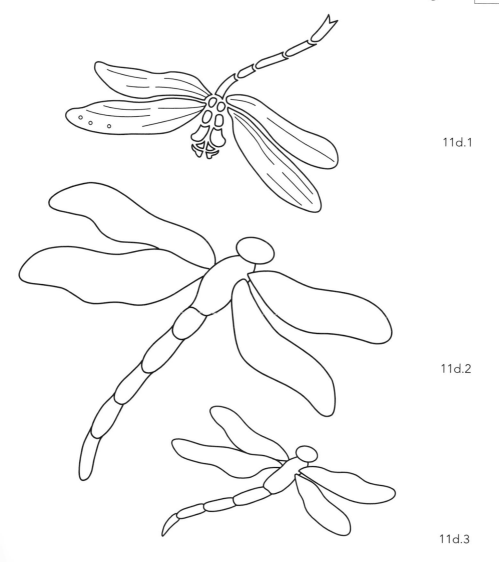

11d.1

11d.2

11d.3

11e.1

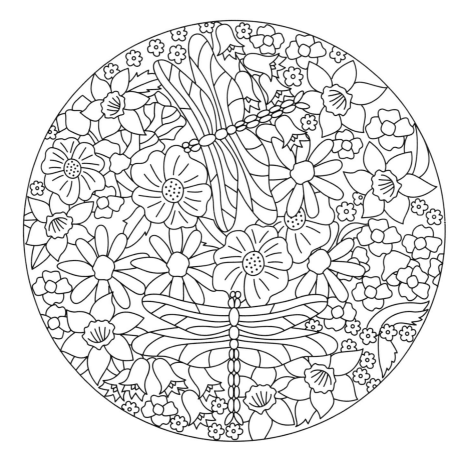

11e.2

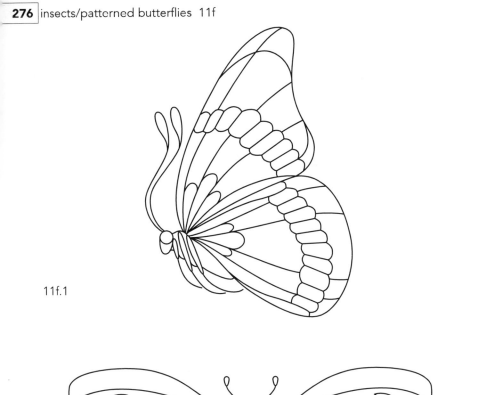

11f.1

11f.2

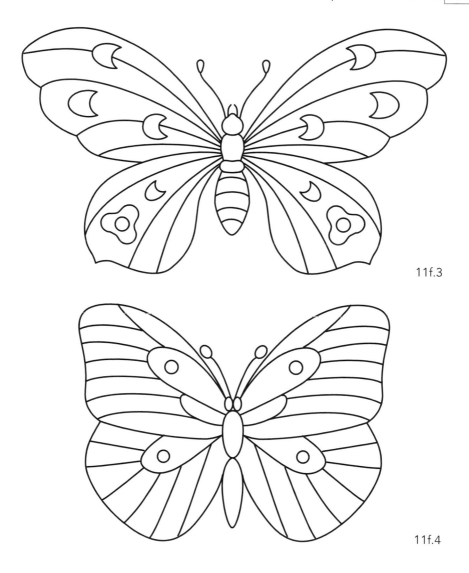

11f.3

11f.4

11f.5

11f.6

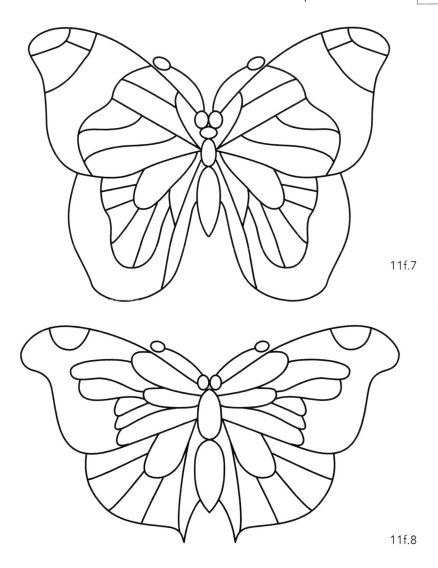

11f.7

11f.8

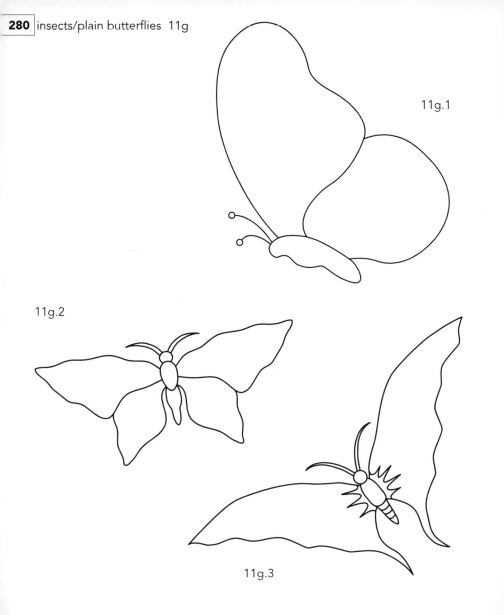

11g.1

11g.2

11g.3

11h.1

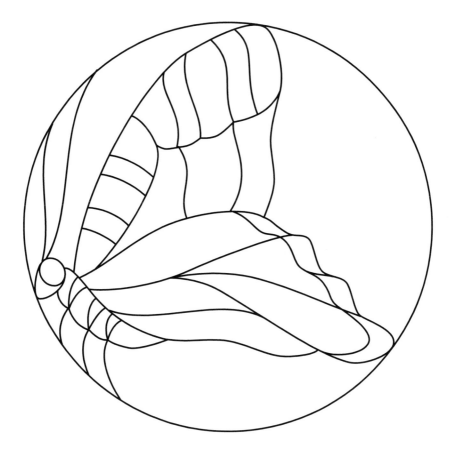

11h.2

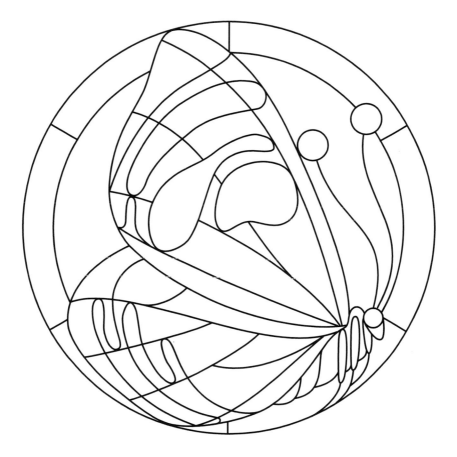

11h.3

11i.1

11i.2

11i.3

11i.4

12.animals

12a.2

12a.1

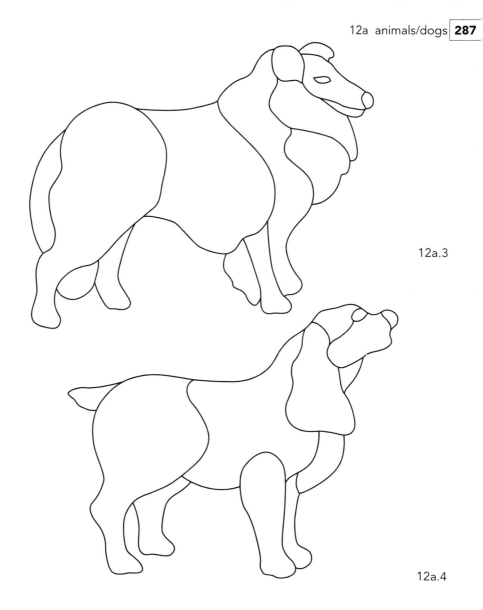

12a.3

12a.4

12b.1

12b.2

12b.3

12c.1

12c.2

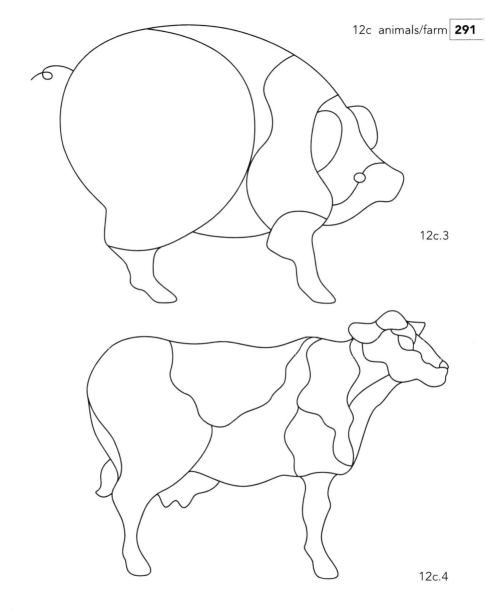

12c.3

12c.4

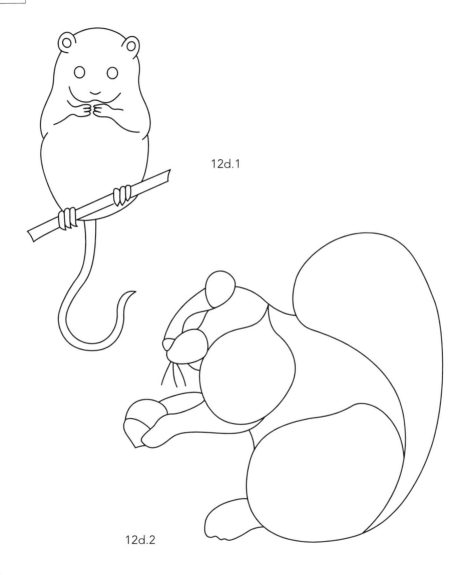

12d.1

12d.2

12d.3

12d.4

12e.1

12e.2

12e.3

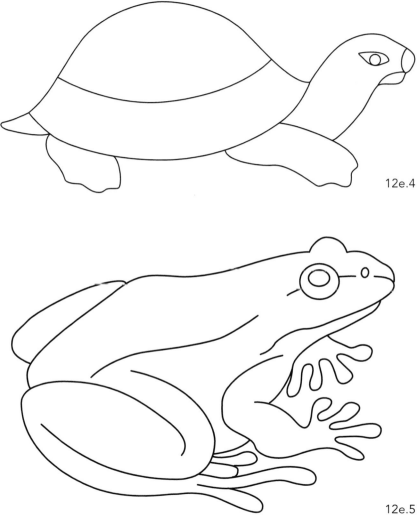

12e.4

12e.5

12f.1

12f.2

12g.1

12g.2

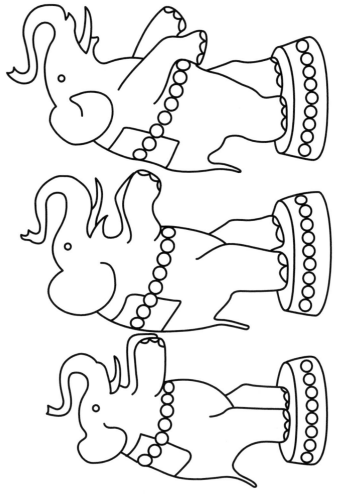

12g.3

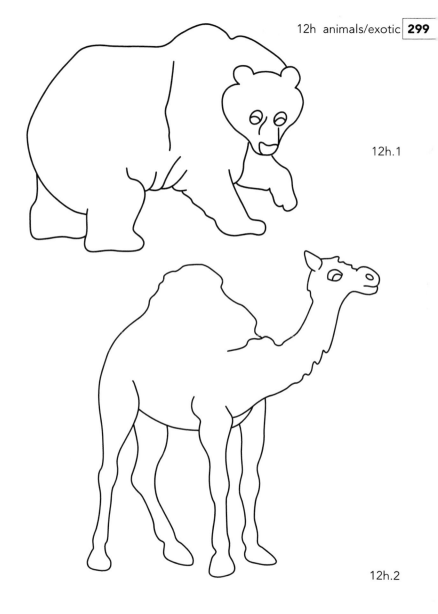

12h.1

12h.2

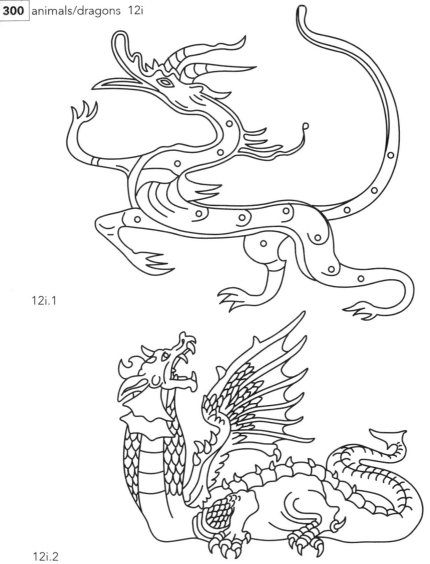

12i.1

12i.2

12i.3

12i.4

12i.5

12i.6

12i.7

12i.8

12i.9

12j.1

12j.2

12j.3

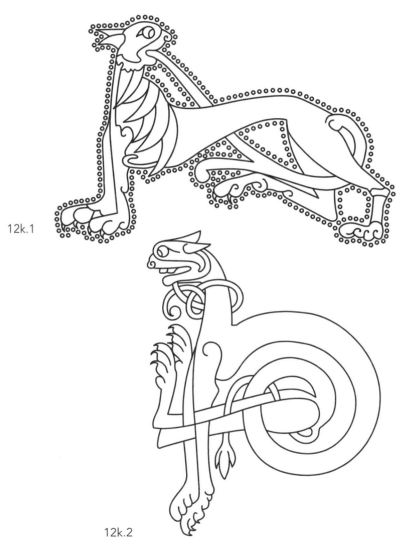

12k.1

12k.2

12l.1

12l.2

12m.1

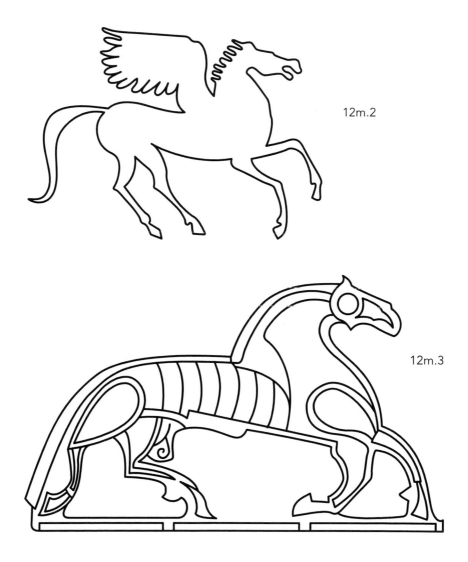

12m.2

12m.3

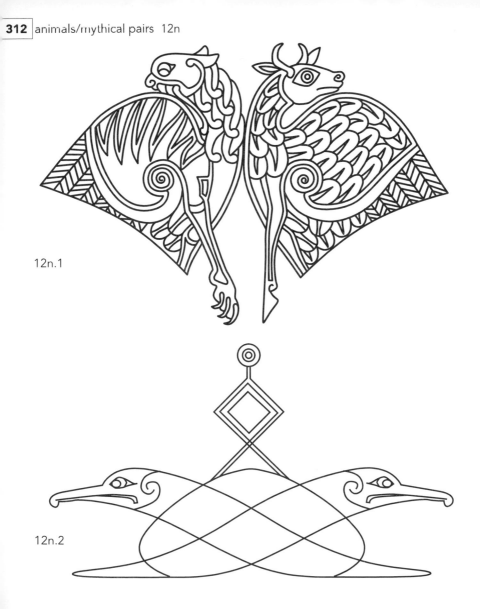

12n.1

12n.2

12n.3

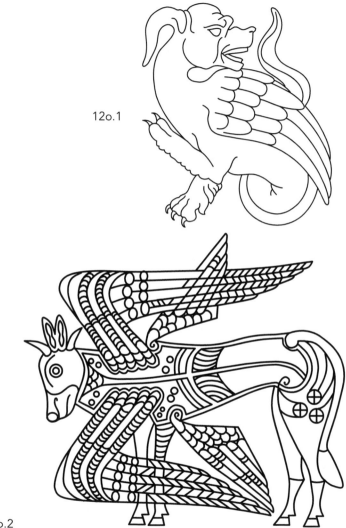

12o.1

12o.2

12o.3

12o.4

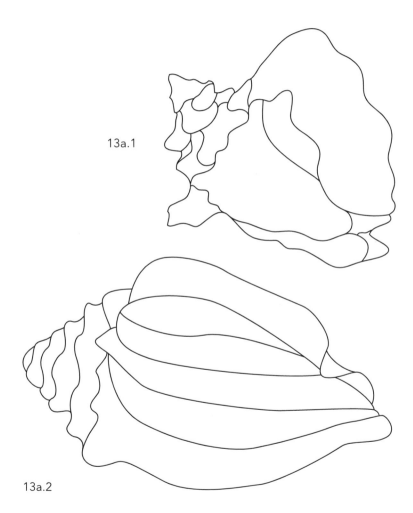

13a.1

13a.2

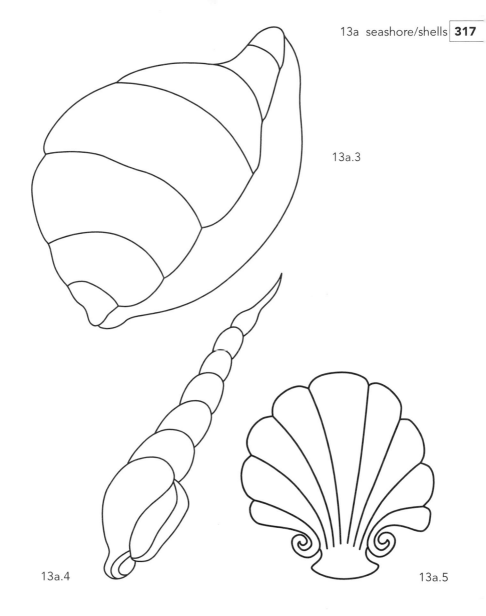

13a.3

13a.4

13a.5

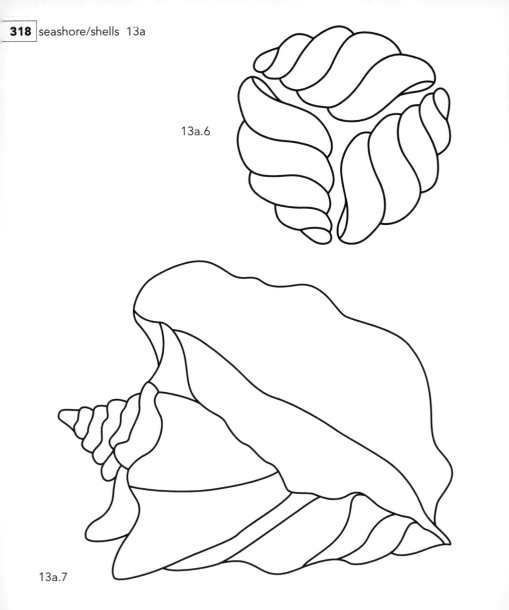

13a.6

13a.7

13b.1

13c.1

13c.2

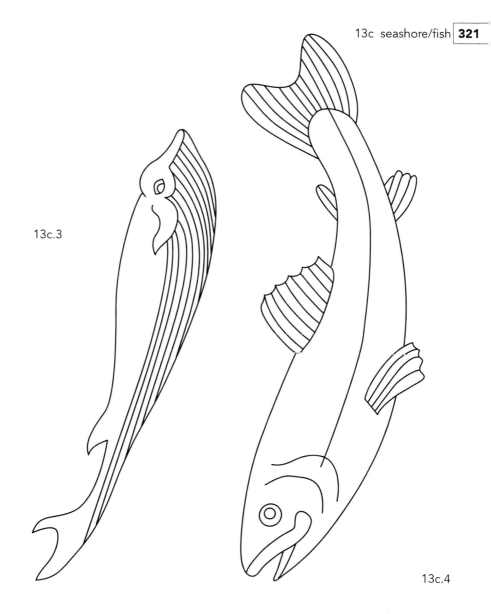

13c.3

13c.4

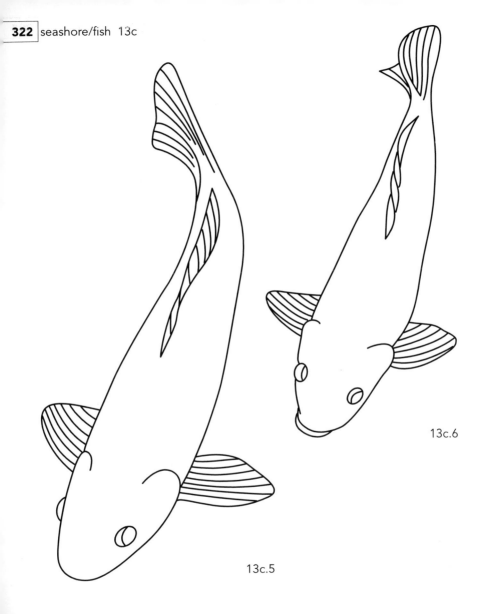

13c.6

13c.5

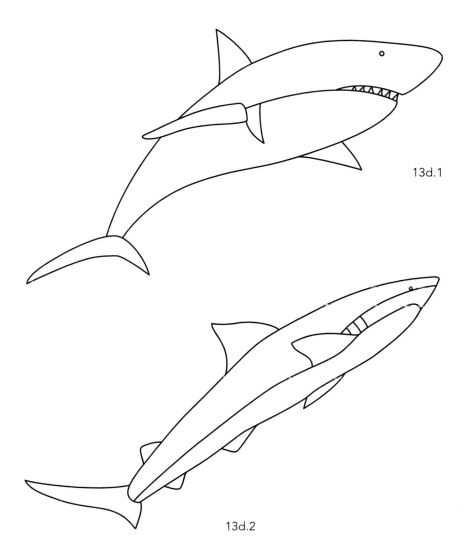

13d.1

13d.2

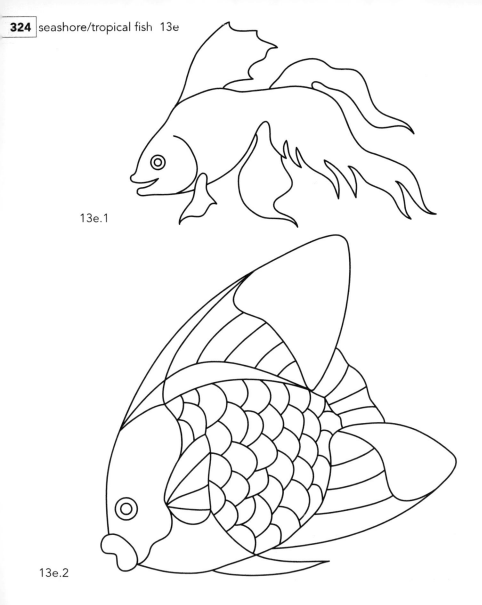

13e.1

13e.2

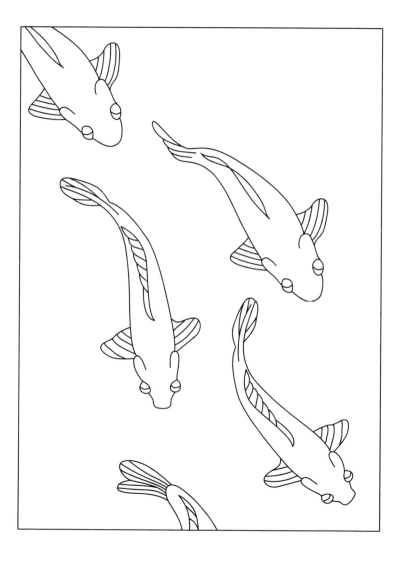

13f.1

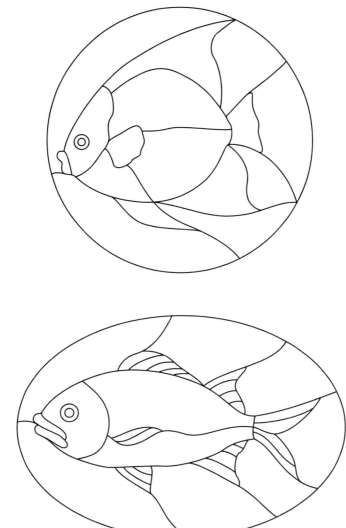

13f.2

13f.3

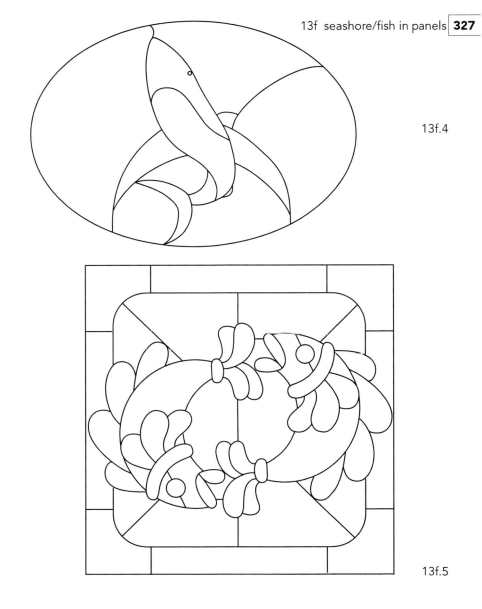

13f.4

13f.5

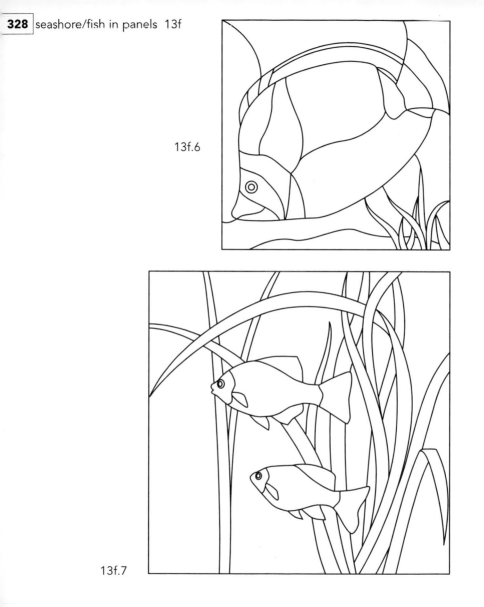

13f.6

13f.7

13f.8

13f.9

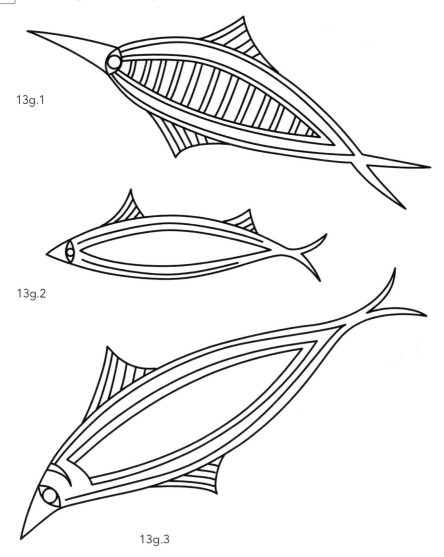

13g.1

13g.2

13g.3

13h.1

13i.1

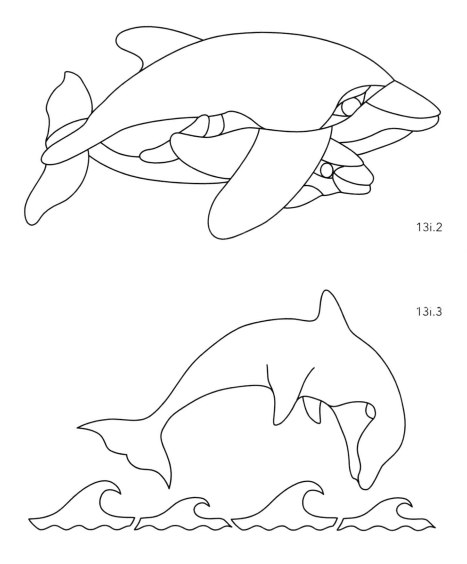

13i.2

13i.3

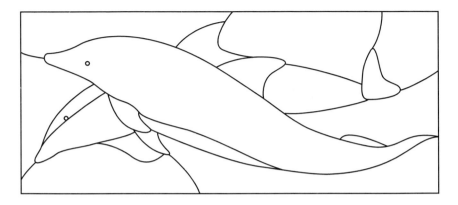

13j.1

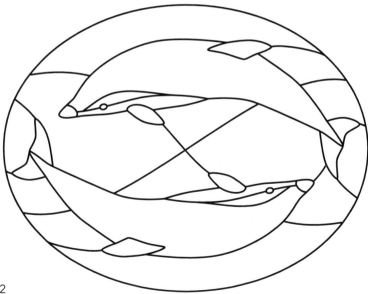

13j.2

13j.3

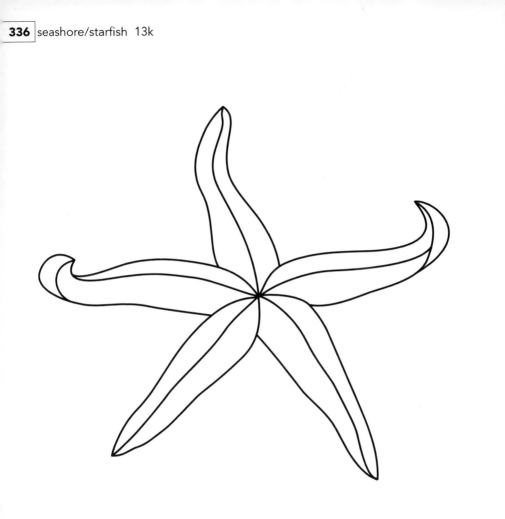

13k.1

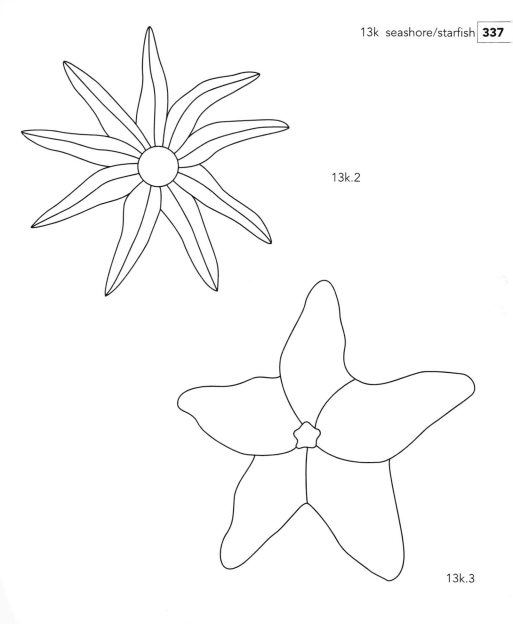

13k.2

13k.3

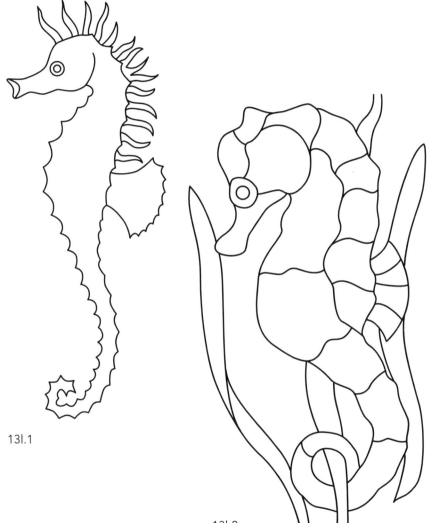

13l.1

13l.2

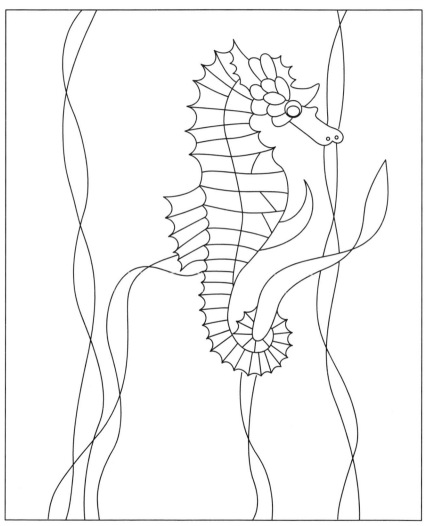

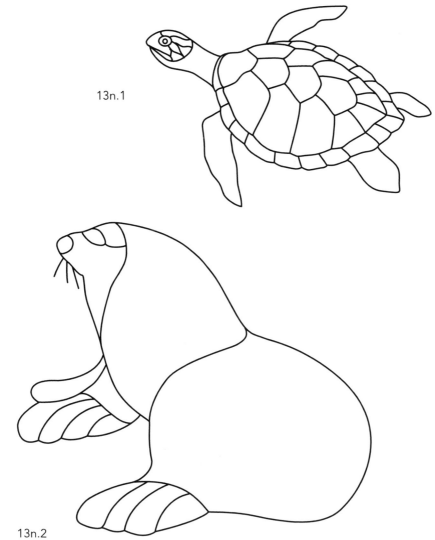

13n.1

13n.2

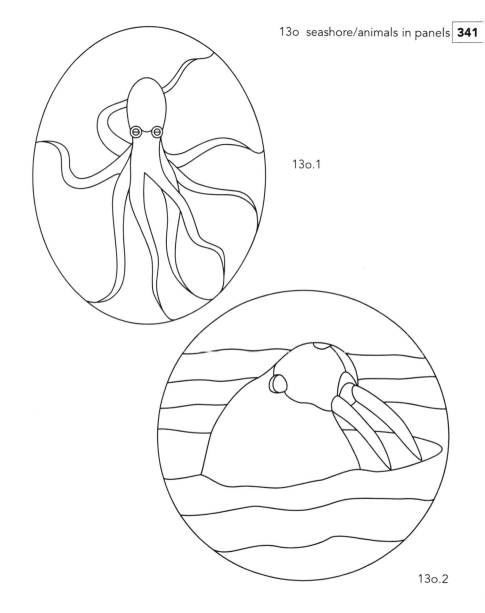

13o.1

13o.2

13p.1

14a.1

14a.2

14a.3

14b.1

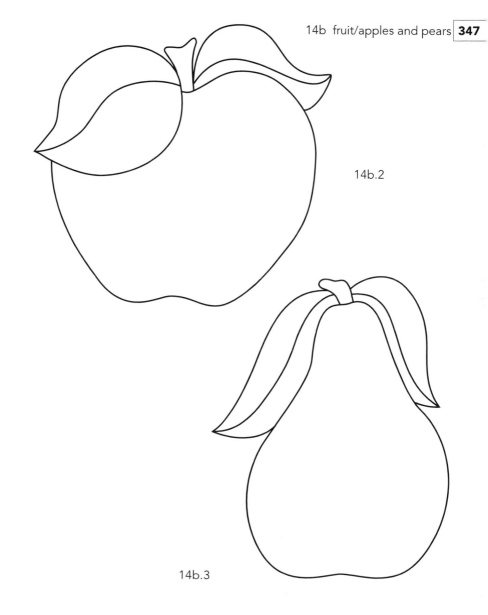

14b.2

14b.3

14b.4

14b.5

14c.1

14c.2

14d.1

14d.2

14d.3

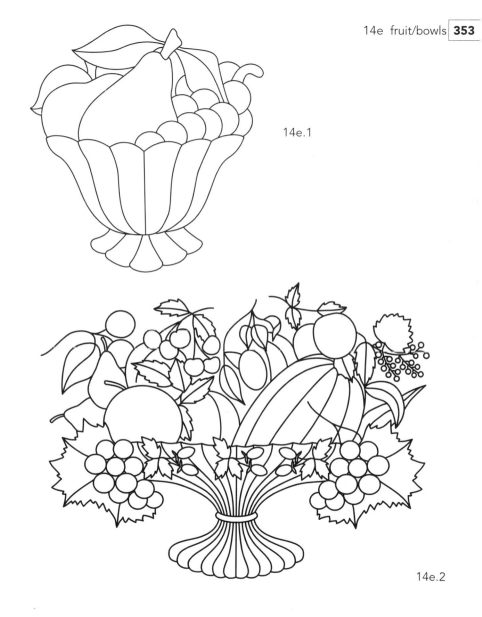

14e.1

14e.2

14f.1

14f.2

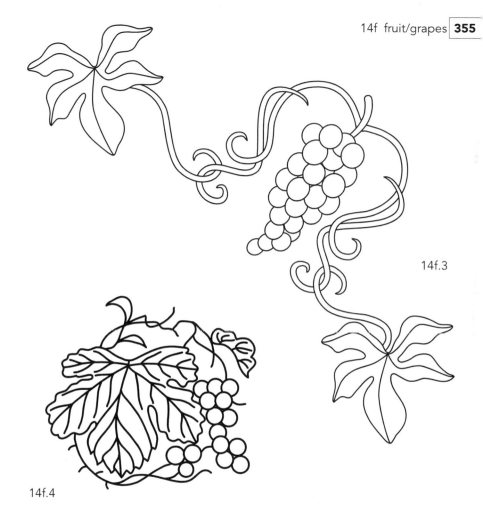

14f.3

14f.4

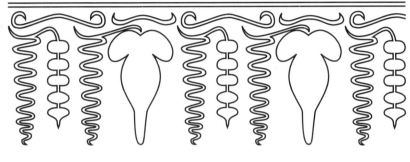

14g.1

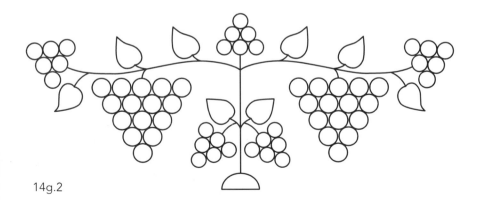

14g.2

14g.3

14g.4

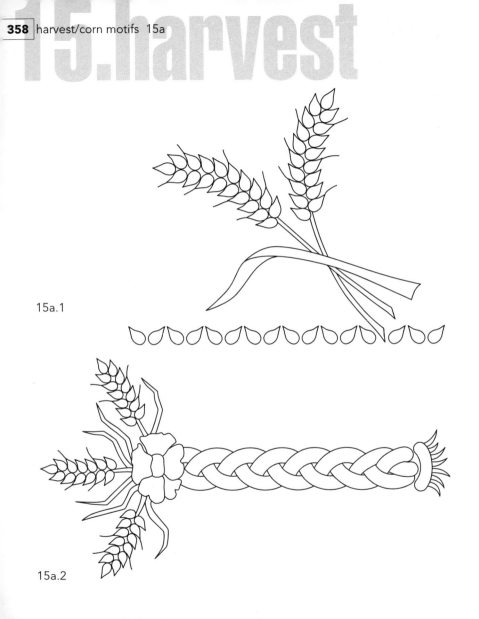

15a.1

15a.2

15b.1

15b.2

15c.1

15c.2

15c.3

15c.4

16a.1

16a.2

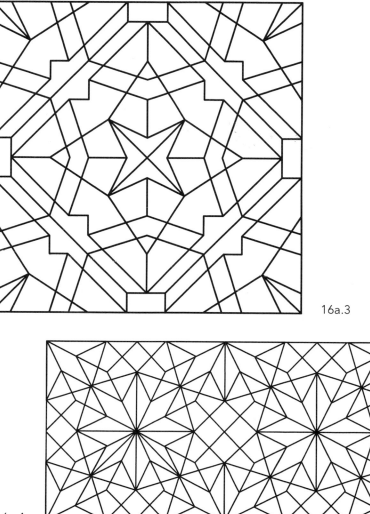

16a.3

16a.4

16a.5

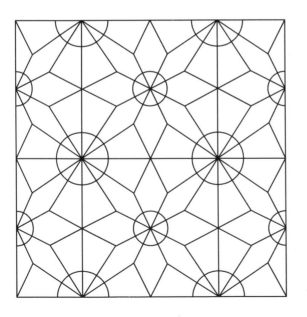

16a.6

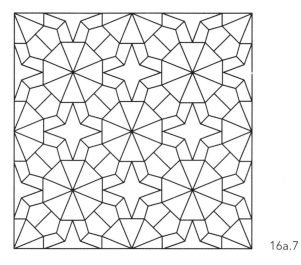

16a.7

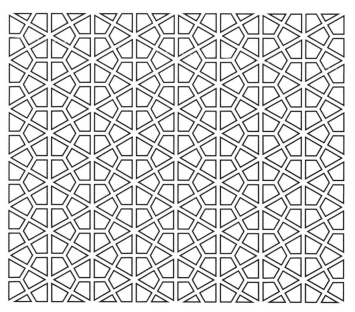

16a.8

16b.1

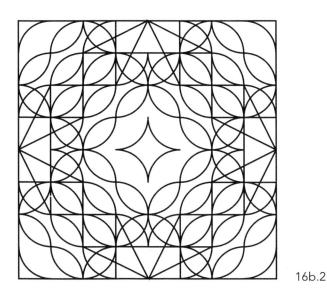

16b.2

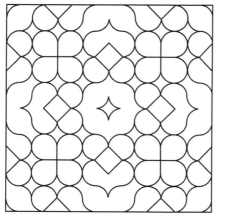

16b.3

16b.4

16c.1

16c.2

16c.3

16c.4

16c.5

16d.1

16d.2

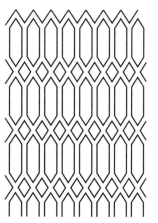

16d.3

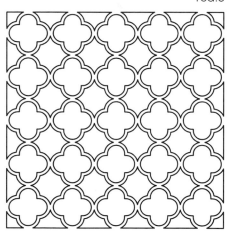

16e.1

16e.2

16e.3

16e.4

16f.1

16f.2

16f.3

16f.4

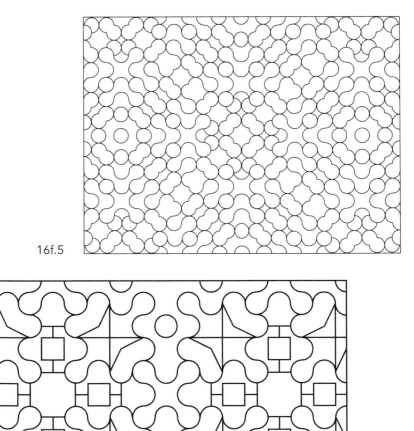

16f.5

16f.6

16f.7

16f.8

17a.1

17a.2

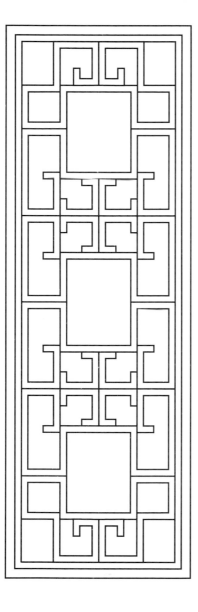

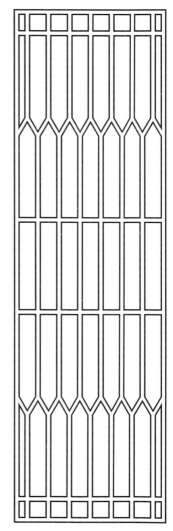

17a.3

17a.4

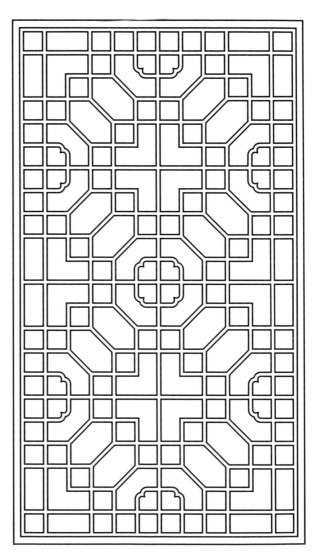

17a.5

17a.6

17a.7

17a.8

17a.9

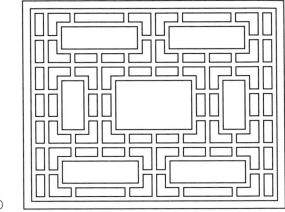

17a.10

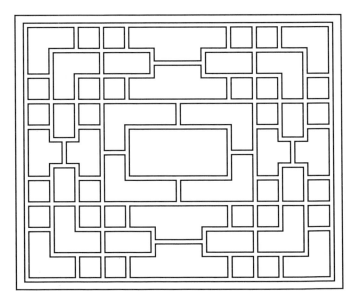

17a.11

17a.12

17a.13

17a.14

17b.1

17b.2

17c.1

17c.2

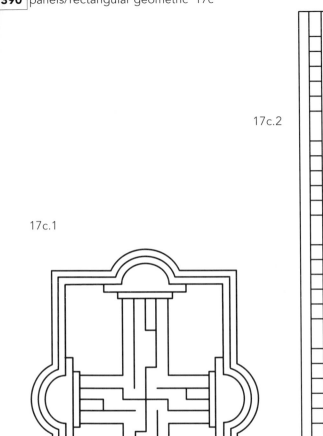

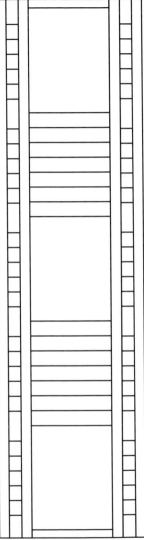

17c.3

17c.4

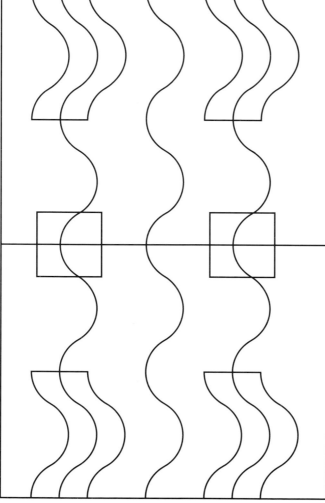

17c.5

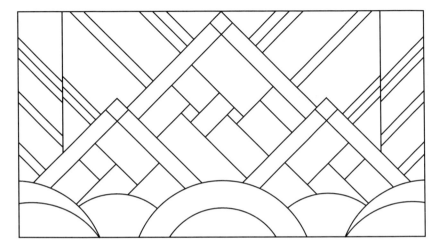

17d.1

17d.2

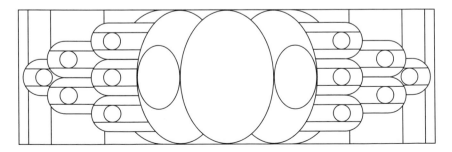

17d.3

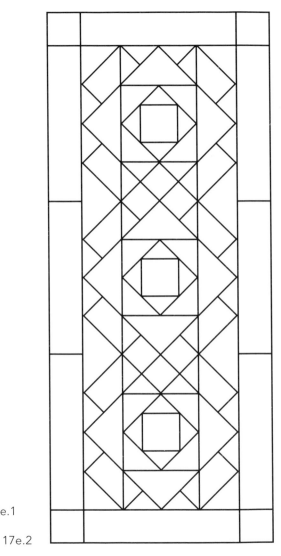

17e.1

17e.2

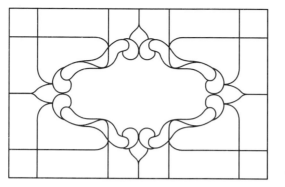

17e.3

17e.4

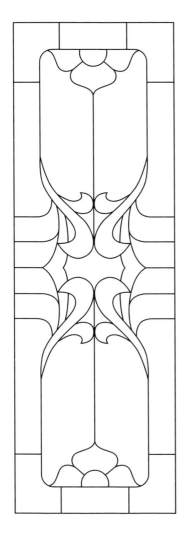

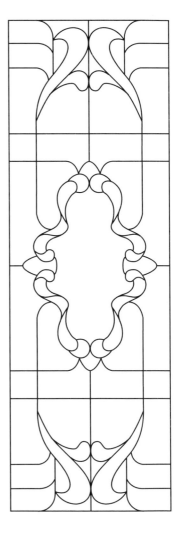

17e.5

17e.6

17e.7

17e.8

17f.1

17f.2

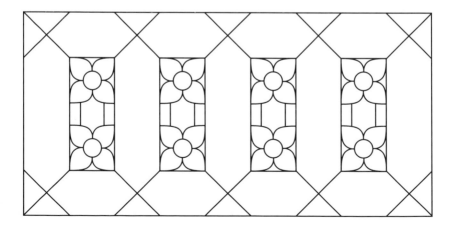

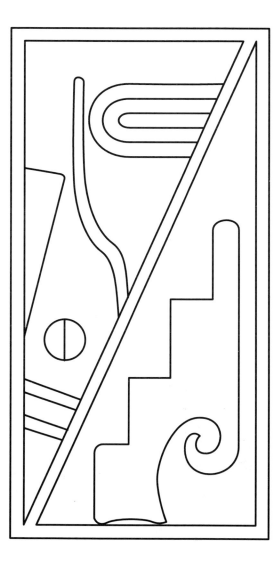

17f.3

17g.1

17g.2

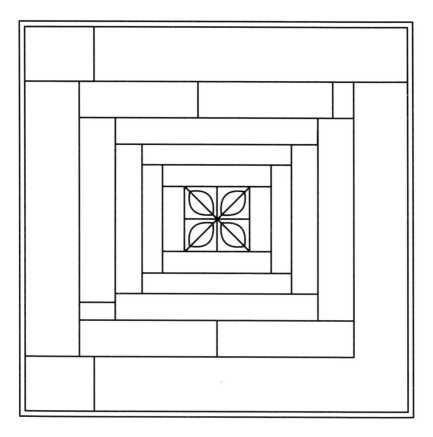

17h.1

17h.2

17h.3

17h.4

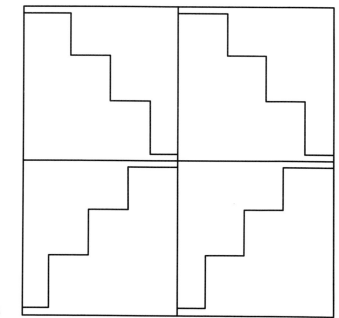

17h.5

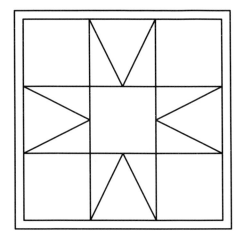

17h.6

17h.7

17i.1

17i.2

17i.3

17j.1

17k.1

17k.2

17k.3

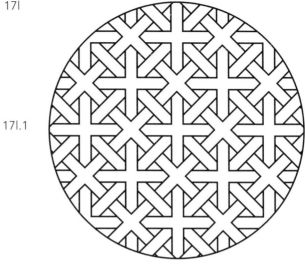

171.1

171.2

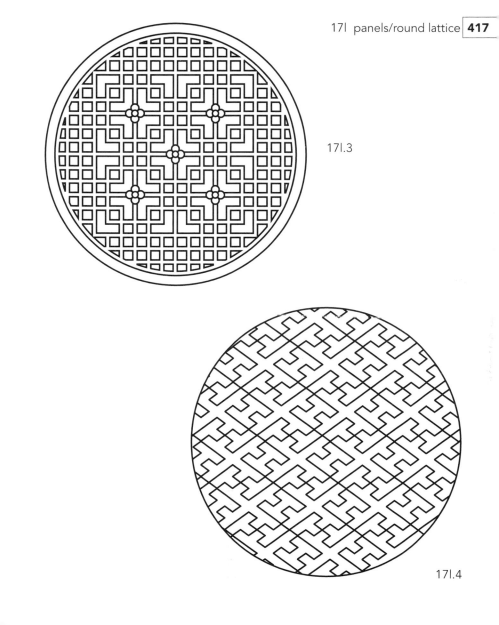

171.3

171.4

171.5

171.6

171.7

17m.1

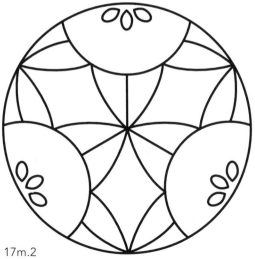

17m.2

17m.3

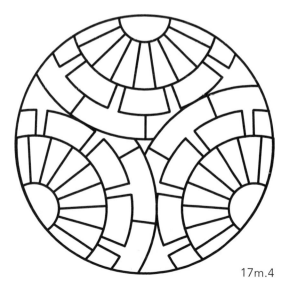

17m.4

17m.5

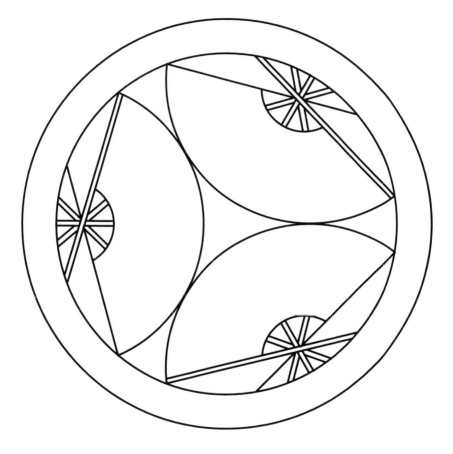

17m.6

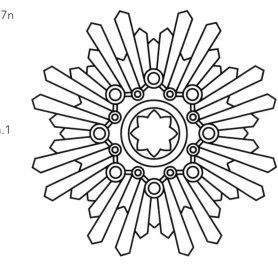

17n.1

17n.2

17n.3

17n.4

17n.5

17n.6

17n.7

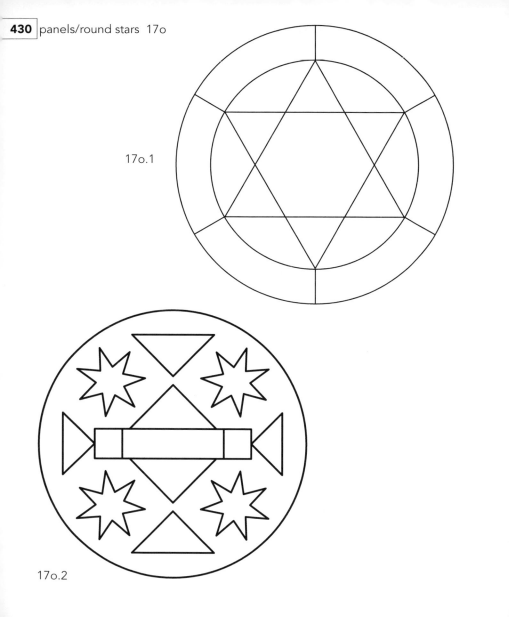

17o.1

17o.2

17p.1

17p.2

17q.1

17q.2

17q.3

17q.4

17q.5

17q.6

17q.7

17q.8

17q.9

17q.10

17q.11

17q.12

17q.13

17r.1

17r.2

17s.1

17s.2

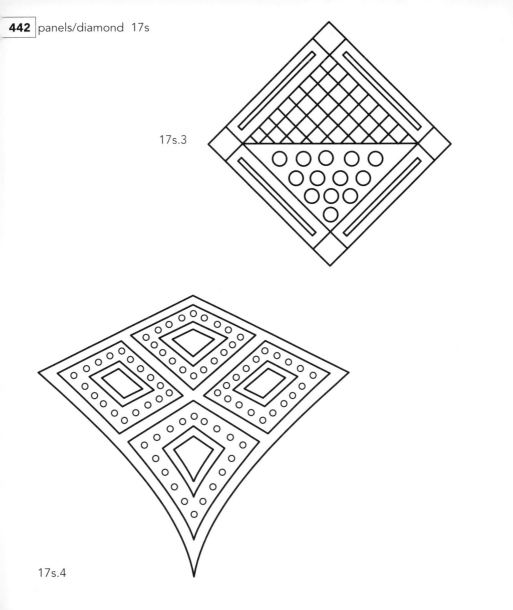

17s.3

17s.4

17s.5

17s.6

17s.7

17s.8

17t.1

17t.2

17t.3

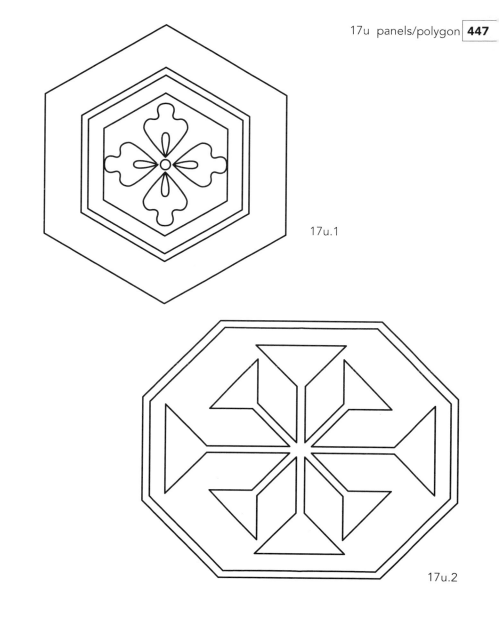

17u.1

17u.2

17v.1

17v.2

17v.3

17v.4

17w.1

17w.2

17w.3

17w.4

17w.5

17w.6

17w.7

17w.8

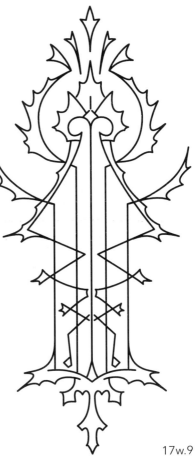

17w.9

17w.10

17w.11

18.knots

18a.1

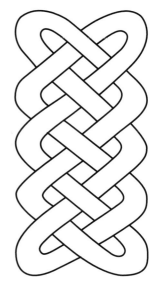

18a.2

18b.1

18b.2

18c.1

18d.1

18d.2

18e.1

18e.2

18e.3

18f.1

18f.2

18g.1

18g.2

18g.3

19.borders

19a.1

19a.2

19a.3

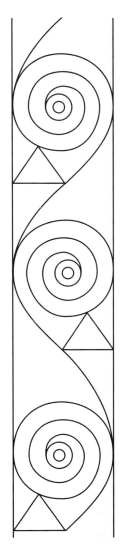

19a.4

19a.5

19a.6

19a.7   19a.8   19a.9

19b.1   19b.2   19b.3

19b.4

19b.5

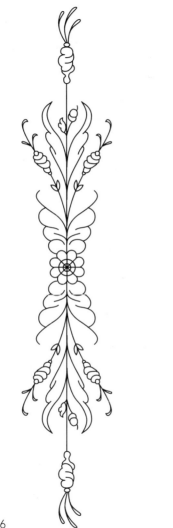

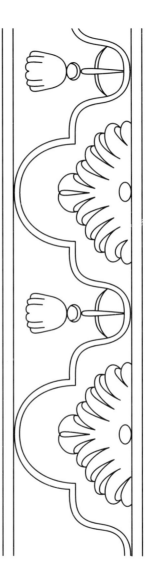

19b.6

19b.7

19b.8

19b.9

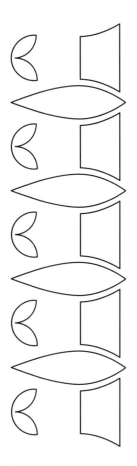

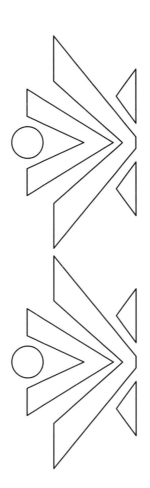

19b.10

19b.11

19b.12

19b.13

19b.14

19b.15

19b.16

19c.1

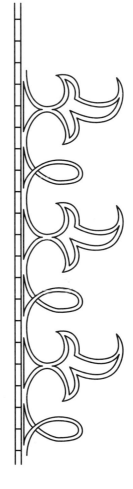

19c.2

19c.3

19c.4

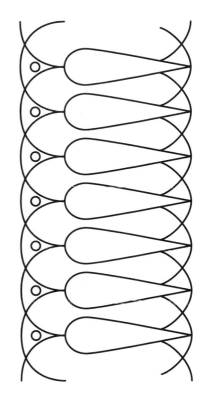

19c.5

19c.6

19c.7

19c.8

19c.9

19c.10

19c.11

19c.12

19c.13

19c.14

19c.15

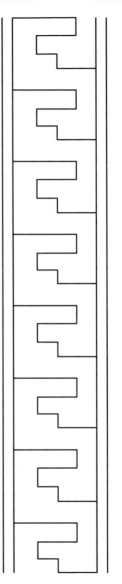

19d.1

19d.2

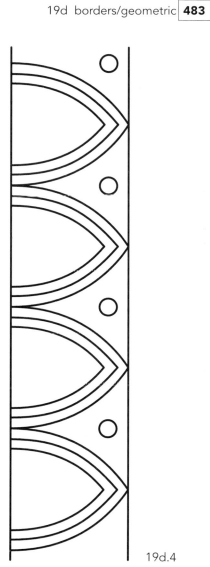

19d.3

19d.4

19e.1

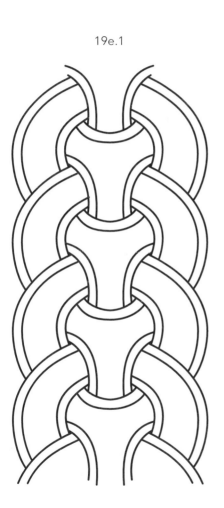

19e.2

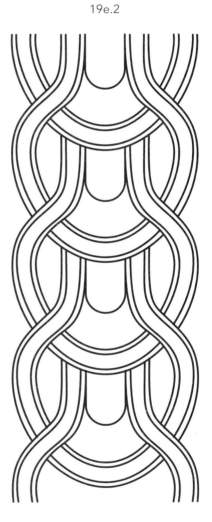

19e.3 19e.4

19f.2

19f.1

19g.1   19g.2

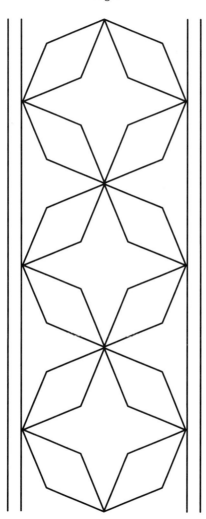
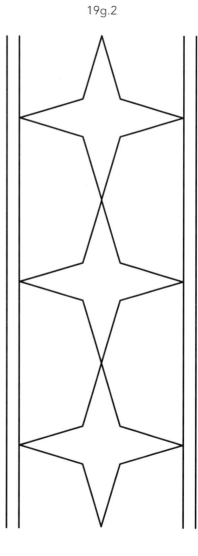

19h.1

19h.2

19h.3

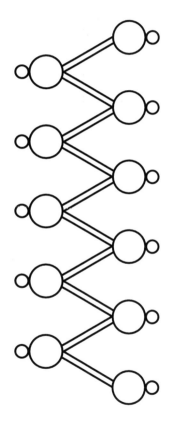

19i.1

19i.2

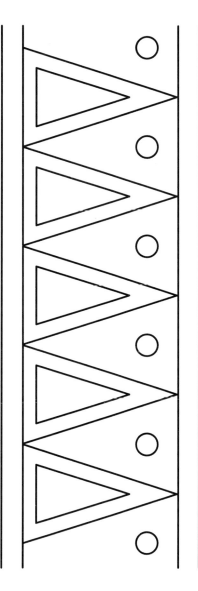

19i.3   19i.4

19j.1

19j.2

19j.3

19j.4

19j.5

19j.6

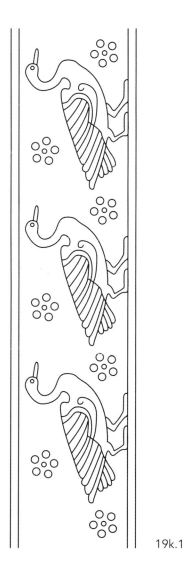

19k.1

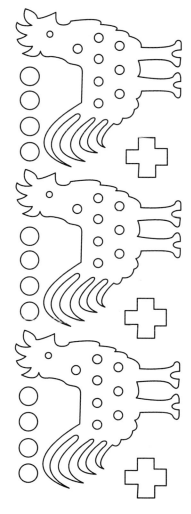

19k.2

191.1

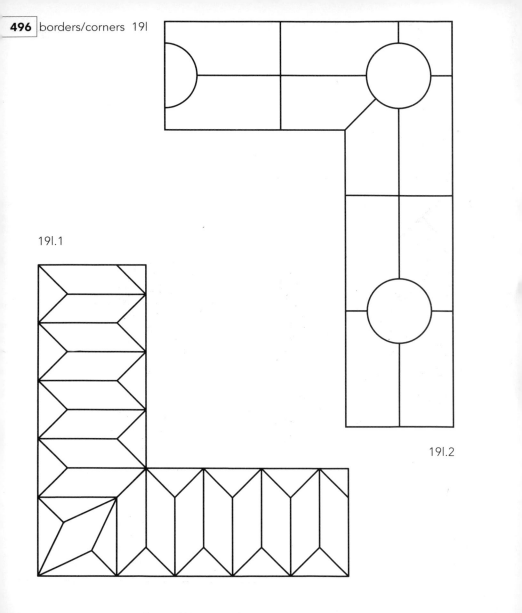

191.2

191.4

191.3

20.banners

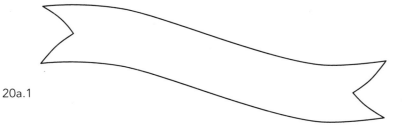

20a.1

20a.2

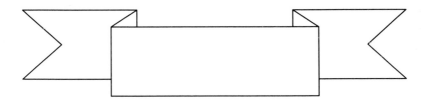

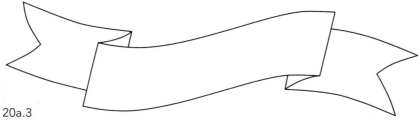

20a.3

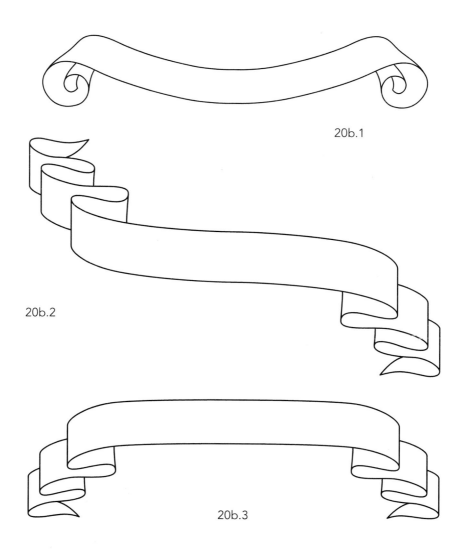

20b.1

20b.2

20b.3

20c.1

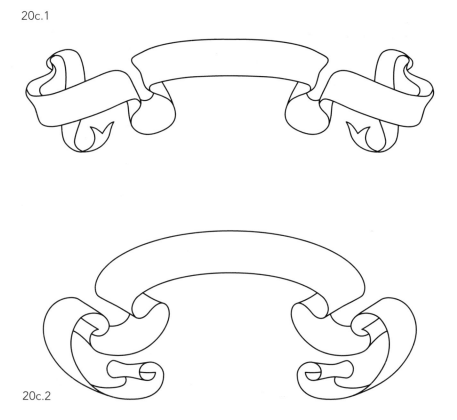

20c.2

20d.1

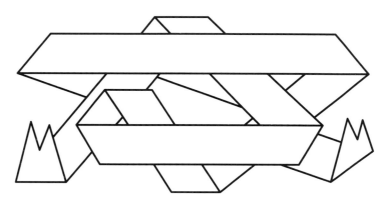

20d.2

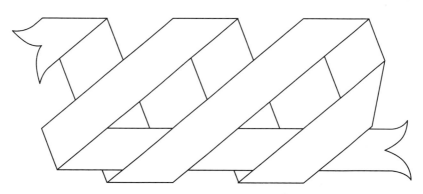

21.frames

21a.1

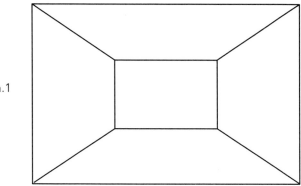

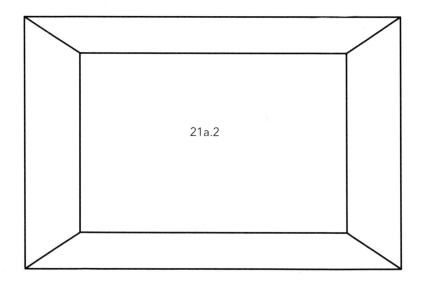21a.2

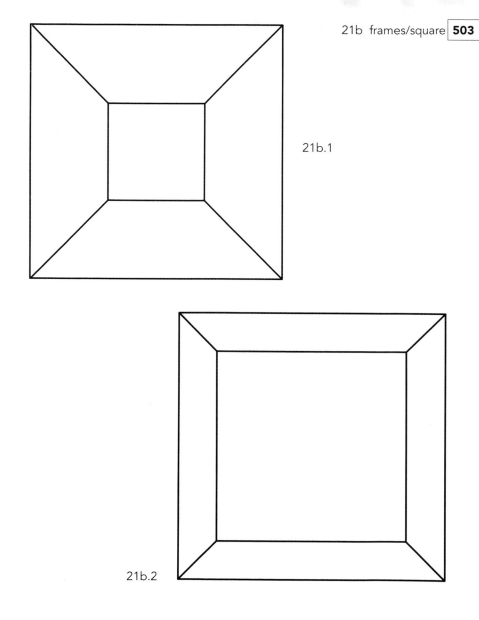

21b.1

21b.2

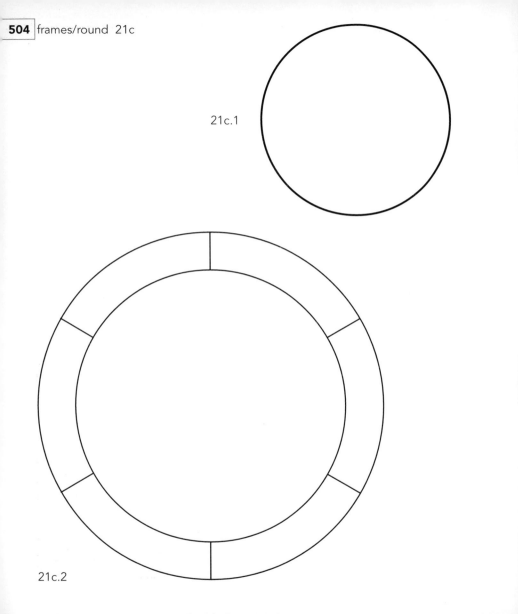

21c.1

21c.2

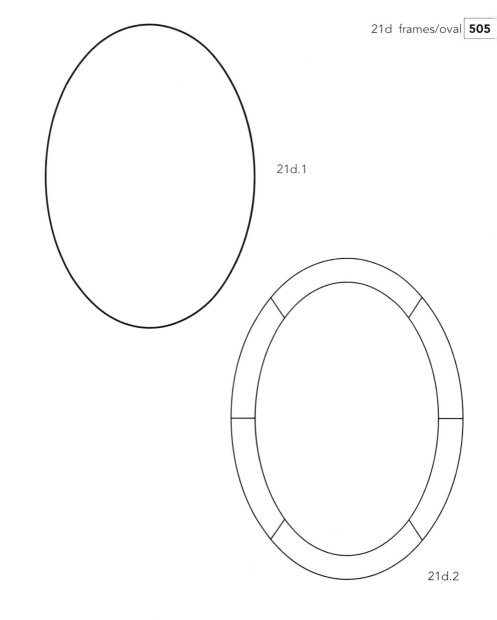

21d.1

21d.2

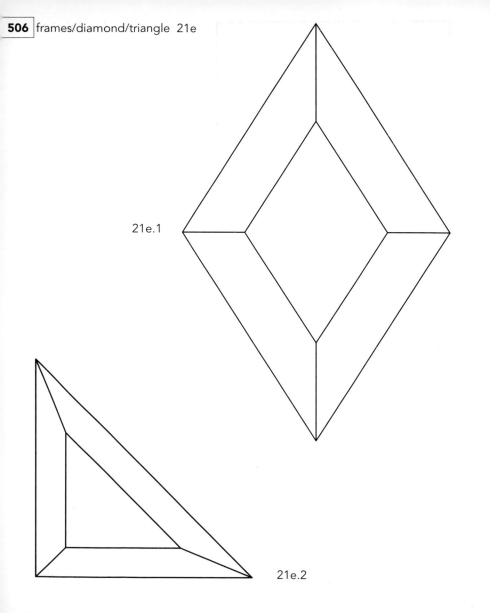

21e.1

21e.2

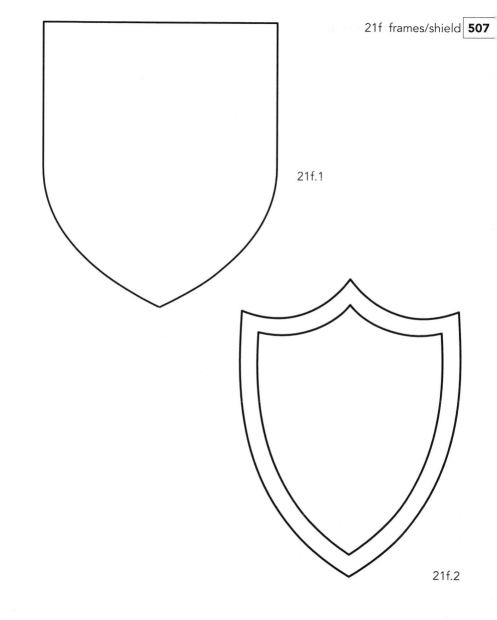

21f.1

21f.2

21g.1

21g.2

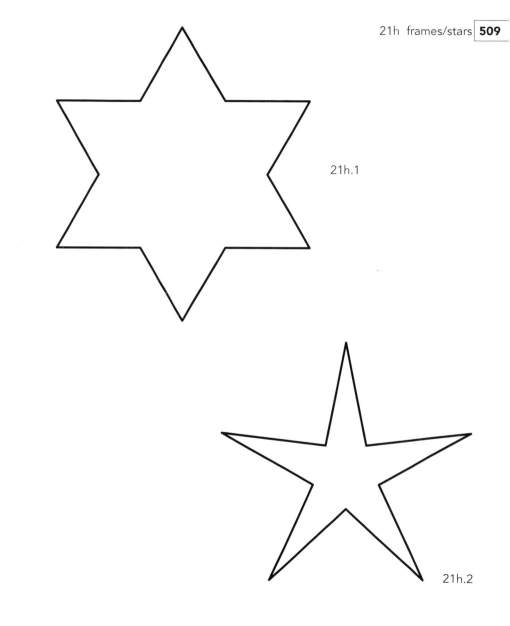

21h.1

21h.2

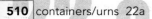

22a.1

22a.2

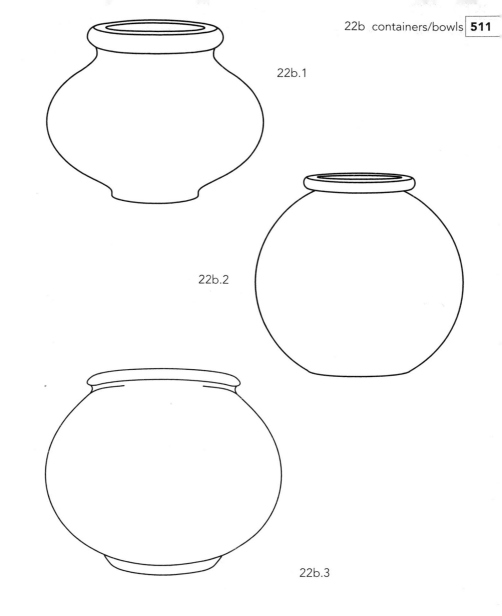

22b.1

22b.2

22b.3

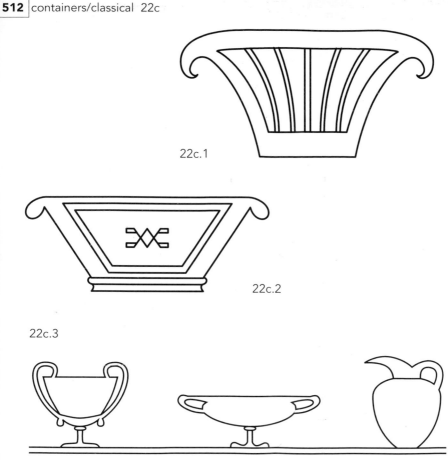

22c.1

22c.2

22c.3

Some motifs in this book have previously appeared in *The Crafter's Pattern Source Book* by Mary McCarthy and *The Complete Guide to Glass Painting* by Alan D. Gear and Barry L. Freestone, both published by Collins & Brown. For more information about Rainbow Glass and its range of products, write to 85 Walkden Road, Worsley, Manchester M28 7BQ. Tel: 0161-790 3025.